TRIATHLONS
FOR
WOMEN

Books by Sally Edwards

Triathlons for Women (1992)
Triathlons for Kids (1992)
Triathlons for Fun (1992)
The Equilibrium Plan (1987)
Triathlon Training and Racing (1985)
The Woman Runner's Training Diary (1984)
The Triathlon Log (1983)
How to Organize a Triathlon (1983)
Triathlon: A Triple Fitness Sport (1982)

TRIATHLONS FOR WOMEN

by Sally Edwards

A Triathlon Book Series

Published by Triathlete Magazine

Library of Congress Cataloging in
Publication Data

First printing: January 1992
Printed in the USA

Triathlete Magazine
Santa Monica, CA

Additional copies may be purchased by
sending a check for $9.00 for shipping
and handling (add applicable state sales
tax) to:

FLEET FEET PRESS
2408 "J" Street
Sacramento, CA 95816
(916) 442-3338

Acknowledgments

My thanks to everyone who works with me on a daily basis for allowing me the liberty to take time from my principal business, *FLEET FEET, Incorporated,* to write this book series. My appreciation goes out to both the owners and managers of the 40 *FLEET FEET* stores as well as to the members of my corporate team: Donna Lee (who spent every free moment doing a spectacular job of editing), Syd Winlock, Hillary Hufford, Julie Hendrickx, Bruce Cannon, and Jody Egan.

Thanks, too, to my reviewers (who are also among my training partners): Ardis Bow, Valerie Doyle, Joyce Flynn, and John Arys.

I would also like to thank all of our female ancestors—in my case, my mom, Gaye Edwards, and my grandmothers, Helen Perry Edwards and Gwendolyn Gaynor Roberts—without whom we as women would not have gotten as far as we have today.

Lastly, my thanks to *Triathlete Magazine* for helping this book come to life and find its way into your hands so that we could get to know one another.

Contents

Let her
Swim,
Climb mountain peaks,
Pilot airplanes,
Battle against the elements,
Take risks,
Go out for adventure,
And
She will not
Feel before the world
... timidity.
      Simone de Beauvoir

1

We're in for the Duration

From Tomboy to Athlete

Our fathers are proud. Our mothers are amazed. We're winning races, finishing marathons, training for triathlons, swimming before work, and touring on our bikes rather than in our cars.

This is the 1990s and women are into sports. There are more women in sports today than at any other time in history, and we are feeling the effects—the enhanced self-esteem, the feelings of achievement, and the joy of excellence. What took us so long?

At the 1991 Danskin Women's Triathlon Series-San Diego, these feelings were alive. As the men stood on the sidelines as support crew and the women competed, there was a feeling of exhilaration and energy in the air. And at the awards ceremony, it was a man who pointed out just how much the basic attitudes about female athletes have changed. In explaining the newfound (and hard-fought) acceptance of women as athletes, the president of the 105-year-old Danskin company, Greg Rorke, said to the hundreds in the audience, "A generation ago you would have been labeled tomboys—you know, women who want to be like men or girls who want to be like boys. But you also know that women love sports the same way that men do. You are each athletes, not tomboys."

Greg Rorke, President of Danskin and founder of the Danskin Women's Triathlon Series (DWTS), during the awards ceremony.

Greg was right. Here was a group of female athletes that a few decades ago would have been stigmatized as "tomboys." I was.

Today we are raising our children as girl and young woman athletes, not as tomboys. The derogatory label has been dropped, and a whole generation of girls are growing up with a vision of themselves as strong, competent, and capable of anything.

That's what I want for each of us, and that's part of what I think triathlon can provide.

The History of Women in Triathlons

Though triathlon has a short history, it is full of colorful tales that capture the imagination and the spirit of sports.

Races such as the Ironman are the best example. In my second (of what are now 13) Ironman completions, I shared a memorable finish-line experience. The year before, in 1981, I had finished second in what is now considered a slow 12 hours and 37 minutes, and a woman from Baltimore named Lyn Brooks had taken third place. In 1982, I knew that she was ahead of me as I started to run the marathon, and I knew that running was her first sport, as it was mine.

Lyn Brooks, the only woman (or man) to complete eleven consecutive Hawaiian Ironmans. October, 1982, Lyn finishes in third place.

After eleven hours spent swimming 2.4 miles and cycling 112 miles, at the fifteen-mile point in the marathon, I caught Lyn. We were both exhausted and reduced to running a fatigue-laden, eight-and-a-half minute per mile pace, so we shuffled along, side by side. It was the first time that we had met—each of us only knew of the other by reputation.

Neither of us had the energy left to compete, so I asked Lyn if she would like to run those last few miles together and tie. Without pause, she agreed, and a wave of relief passed over me. I'll never forget those last few miles together, running, sweating, and frying under the Hawaiian sun that gave no mercy. That day Lyn and I shared something that is difficult to find in most places in life—the mutual respect, trust, and love that athletes experience when they have given their all in pursuit of self-accomplishment and the finish line.

We ended up tying for third, with a final time of 11 hours and 51 minutes, almost one hour faster than our times had been the year before. In fact, our 1982 time was fast enough to *win* the 1981 race. Lyn and I were obviously not the only ones who were improving their times.

Indeed, the toppling of finish-time records in women's triathlon has been a consistent phenomenon, and we have come a long way very quickly. When Paula Newby-Fraser broke the course record with a 9:01 in 1988, few ignored the fact that no man had broken 9:01 before 1983. And, with each passing year, the times continue to drop.

Year	Ironwoman Winners	Masters Champions
1979	Lyn Lemaire 12:55:38	None
1980	Robin Beck 11:21:24	None
1981	Linda Sweeney 12:00:32	None
1982	Kathleen McCartney (F)* 11:09:40	Barbara Shubert 14:01:16
1982	Julie Leach (O) 10:54:08	Barbara Shubert 12:22:20
1983	Sylviane Puntous 10:43	Linda Keeney 12:59:06
1984	Sylviane Puntous 10:25:13	Marcia Barnett 12:42:27
1985	Joanne Ernst 10:25:22	Joan Dunn 12:03:26
1986	Paula Newby-Fraser 9:49:14	Leslie Cens-McDowell 12:05:03
1987	Erin Baker 9:35:25	Sally Edwards 11:07:52
1988	Paula-Newby Fraser 9:01:01	Leslie Cens-McDowell 11:22:43
1989	Paula Newby-Fraser 9:00:56	Karen Smith-Rohrberg 10:56:56
1990	Erin Baker 9:13:42	Leslie Cens-McDowell 11:17:36
1991	Paula Newby-Fraser 9:07:52	Sally Edwards 11:09:13

There were two races in 1982, due to the fact that the race was rescheduled that year from a spring to a fall event.

Triathlon stands out in the history of sports; from its inception female triathletes have been accepted as bona fide competitors, not as members of a second-class sideshow. Compare this with track, where women were barred from competing in anything longer than 200 meters until the 1960 Olympic Games, because the International Olympic Commission decreed that greater distances were too strenuous for the female constitution. The women's 3,000-meter run wasn't even added to the Olympics until 1984, the same year the women's marathon was first included as an Olympic sport.

From triathlon's beginnings, women have been in for the duration—the long haul and even the hard crawl.

There were two Bud Light Ironman races in 1982, one in February and another in October, as the race was officially repositioned as a fall event. The February race is especially memorable. After suffering from severe dehydration and exhaustion, Julie Moss crumpled to the ground 15 yards from the finish line, and, moments before she crossed on her hands and knees, Kathleen McCartney passed her for the first-place victory. ABC television captured the moment and televised it across the world as one of the most heroic finishes ever in the history of sports. Many current Ironpeople have said that watching Julie crawl those last yards so inspired them that they decided to take up the sport. In 1987, the scene was replayed as Jan Ripple crawled across the finishline, suffering in the same way, and an amazing moment of combined abasement and victory was again presented to the world.

The "Big Four": Patricia and Sylviane Puntous, Erin Baker, and Paula Newby-Fraser have dominated the women's division of triathlon for the past five years. Patricia and Sylviane Puntous, identical twins from Canada, are among the women who have proven that longevity on the professional circuit is possible. In 1987, an epic race was staged when 1983 and 1984 Ironwoman winner Sylviane was left behind in the last miles of the race by New Zealander Erin Baker. The following year, the world of triathlon was again stunned, when Zimbabwe's Paula Newby-Fraser shattered the old Ironwoman record, taking 35 minutes off Baker's time and setting a new world mark of nine hours and one minute. The Ironwomen's race will never be the same again, as her performance would have placed her in 10th place among the men. Newby-Fraser has continued to garner the recognition she deserves, and in 1990 she was named professional woman athlete of the year by the Women's Sports Foundation. In 1991, she won again, an unprecedented fourth victory.

Women have played roles in triathlon other than that of athlete, having been central in the leadership of the sport from its beginnings. Pioneers such as Lyn Brooks and I volunteered endless hours organizing the Triathlon Federation/USA,

Flo Bryan has been one of the leaders in the sport of triathlon, serving as an officer of both Tri Fed/USA and the ITU (International Triathlon Union) Women's Commission. She has also organized over 100 triathlons as the Vice President of CAT Sports.

America's national governing body of triathlon. Internationally, Sara Springman has served in a similar role, working to develop and enhance the position of women in the European arena.

Directorship in the sport has also been a woman's role. The Hawaii Ironman has had a woman, Valerie Silk, at its helm for over a decade. Silk brought ABC's "Wide World of Sports," prize money, and an international circuit to the event that she founded, owned, and later sold. Flo Bryan, vice-president of CAT Sports, has driven the 11 city BLTS Series (formerly the United States Triathlon Series) to its premier place today as well.

Sponsorships, too, have been cultivated by women. The Budweiser brewing company's sponsorship, the key source of capital in triathlon's formulative years, was orchestrated by Jane Marks, whose vision of aligning a beer product with a lifestyle sport was squarely on the mark.

On the technical side, the first computerized timing program, which produces "split times" (including transition times) was developed by Bonnie Miller (Joseph) in 1982.

Clearly, a woman's place in triathlon is in the race—whether as a triathlete, organizer, director, or engineer.

Triathlon has rapidly expanded in America, with women-only events emerging as a well-respected tradition. A women-only triathlon was first held at Marine World Africa USA in 1982, sponsored by Bonnie Bell, the skin care and cosmetics company which also sponsored a national 10k running series. In 1990, Danskin, the 105-year-old women's dancewear company, un-veiled a new line of broad-spectrum women's athletic apparel and sponsored a three-city national triathlon series in support of their efforts. In 1992, the Danskin Triathlon Series expanded to cover seven cities and is the premier women-only event at this time.

Triathlon in Europe has grown in a fashion similar to the United States. As European multi-triathlon champion Sarah Springman, a professional triathlete with a doctoral degree in engineering who teaches at Cambridge University, explains, "Triathlon arrived in Europe in 1982, with the first Nice Triathlon." By 1984, Springman and her all-female team were competing in the London-to-Paris Triathlon (which consisted of a swim across the English Channel, individual 30-mile cycling time trials, a fifty-mile team time trial to Paris, and a marathon run by a relay team of four). Finishing in 10th place out of 16 mostly male teams, Ironwoman Springman writes that triathlon "...rearranged some male egos and impressions of triathlon women."

European women face difficulties not unlike women elsewhere, as Springman verifies, saying, "The elite women receive absolutely no help from their associations or self-seeking coaches." By 1990, though, through the support of the ITU (International Triathlon Union, the international governing body of triathlon) and its president, Les McDonald, women began organizing themselves to support equality of opportunity and participation. At the 1990 ITU World Championships, the "Women's Commission," formed and spearheaded by Lyn Brooks (ITU Technical Director and the same woman who accompanied me to a third place finish in 1982), Flo Bryan and Sarah Springman (Co-Chairs), and Loreen Barnett, passed eight resolutions supporting equality of opportunity and reward for all women. I recommend taking a look ahead to page 150 to read these resolutions now.

Internationally, women's triathlon is growing through the

grassroots efforts of women triathletes and the support of their male counterparts. Some of the women who have stepped forward to lead the movement include: Simone Mortier, Germany; Loreen Barnett, Canada; Dr. Louise Burke, Australia; Ruth Hunt, Hong Kong; Saeko Shimoji and Tomoko Takeuchi, Japan; Fernanda Keller, Brazil; Anne Kelly, France; Dr. Sarah Springman, Great Britain; Lyn Brooks, USA; Marisol Casada, Spain; and Dr. Andrea Sipos, Hungary.

At the pre-race party several nights before 1990's Ironman, Mike Plant, the master of ceremonies, honored all those who were seasoned triathletes, as is his tradition. He asked everyone who had finished the Hawaii event five times or more to stand. Hundreds of the 1,350 entrants stood. Then, slowly, he asked everyone to sit who had not finished the race six times. Dozens lowered themselves into their chairs. Then, Mike asked those who hadn't finished seven times, then eight, then nine, then 10 times, to sit down.

There were two individuals left standing.

Lyn Brooks stood. Tom Warren, the men's 1978 winner, stood.

Mike then asked anyone who had not finished 11 times to sit.

Tom sat, Lyn stood.

After a decade of never missing an Ironman, the woman who tied with me for third place is still racing what is considered one of the toughest races in the world.

Both she and Tom again finished that year. I know Lyn—she'll be back the next year, and she will be the solitary figure left standing at the end of Mike's rite, in an audience of thousands, in an event that circles the globe, in a race that compares to no other.

The Five Answers to the Five Basic Questions

#1. Who? Who should participate in this triple-fitness sport?
Answer: Anyone who wants to.

If you don't want to, then don't. But if you want to have some fun, get fit, and meet some new people who are interested in the same kinds of things, then triathlons might be just right for you.

#2. How? How do I start, and how do I keep it all together and not quit?
Answer: It isn't going to be easy, but it's doable.

You've taken a right step by reading this book, and, if you start to slide back, grab this copy and reread it; I wrote it to motivate you.

This is your life, and this is your agenda; it's not like starting a diet or a car. Starting diets only leads to failure, because in the long run they only change what you eat, not what you do. It's also not like starting a car, where all you do is slide in the ignition key and stomp on the gas pedal. This is, if you do it right, a lifetime fitness program and a serious and rewarding commitment of will.

#3.When? When am I going to find time for all of this training, when I am already busy?
Answer: If there's a will, there's time. Prioritize and organize your time according to your beliefs and goals.

You aren't reading this book or training for triathlons because you are bored or because there is nothing else to do in your life. You are probably reading it because you want more— more challenges, more information, more motivation. If there is a place for fitness in your life, there is time for tri-training. It isn't easy, and you may have to make some trade-offs, but when you make your health your first priority and when you know that being physically fit is the foundation of your health, training becomes quite important enough to make time for.

Most people see tri-training as impossible because they think it's so time-consuming and strenuous. They're wrong. When you make the transition from your current work-out program there will be no greater time requirements than you have already. Designing a swim-bike-run training program will not only be more fun and challenging, it needn't cost you any additional time. If you don't believe me, skip ahead and read the chapters on training.

#4. Where? Where do I train, meet people, learn more, etc.?
Answer: The answers to these questions are all around you.

Network through your local resources. In most communities there are bike, swim, run, and triathlon retail stores that can connect you with people. There are sports clubs—Y's, athletic clubs, and health clubs—that you can join. There are organizations and magazines available to you (see the Appendix for a complete listing). The network is already there—join it.

#5.What? What do I have to do to compete in and complete a triathlon?

Answer: You need to combine the three components to athletic success: efficient biomechanics (how your body moves), proper equipment, and a training plan.

In the following sections, each of the three triathletic sports—swim, bike, and run—will be presented, along with their components, in order for you to build a solid triathletic foundation that will support you through training, competition, and a lifetime of fitness.

2

The Basic Moves—Swimming

Swim Biomechanics

For practical reasons, the only stroke used in triathlons is the freestyle (also known as the "crawl"). The breaststroke, the backstroke, the butterfly, and others simply are not as efficient or as quick as the freestyle.

Think of the body as a lever system—the bones are straight lines, like rigid sticks, and the joints are hinges, like the hinges that swing doors open and closed. Pictured this way, the body is a stick figure with the joints as places around which the sticks rotate.

In the biomechanics of swimming, your job is simple—move your sticks around their hinges, by contracting the right muscles at the right time. This is obviously extremely simplified. Kinesiologists would love to turn this discussion into one about torques, first-, second-, and third-class levers, angles of pull and resistance, pulleys, and equations dealing with power. For our uses, though, the sticks and hinges model will work fine.

When you swim and are thinking in terms of putting together the various movements of your stroke, visualize this stick figure and break down the freestyle into the individual movement of each stick part, as follows:

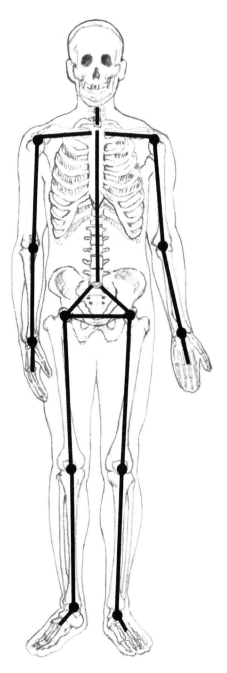

Lever System of the Human Body

The Big Stick: Body Position

The more streamlined your sticks are, the less resistance they will cause and the faster you will move. Compared to a fish, humans aren't very streamlined. There is, though, a lot that we can do with the positioning of our limbs to reduce our bodies' "drag" against the water.

The most basic directive is to always lie as flat as possible, with your body parallel to the surface of the water. Your head and chest will be slightly higher than your legs and ankles though, so that you can kick. The water should cross your face at the hairline, and your shoulders will be at right angles to the line of the body.

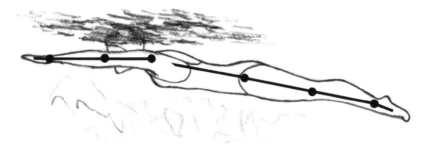

As you breathe through your mouth, twist your neck hinge on its axis, without changing your body position (in simple english, don't lift your head). Your head creates a trough or hole in the water called a bow wave. After you rotate your head, breathe in when your mouth is inside the bow wave.

Just as cars go out of alignment and need to be straightened, so do swimmers. The three common body alignment mistakes and diagnoses are as follows:

Mistake #1 The body is not flat enough in the water.

Diagnosis Failure to maintain a level position is usually caused by:
- trying to lift the head too high, with a resulting drop of the lower body
- not kicking sufficiently, which results in the dropping of the lower body.

Mistake #2 The body moves sideways (laterally).

Diagnosis • Lateral movement can have two causes:
- moving the head out of alignment, which tends to force the body sideways

- lateral movement of the arms, rather than vertcal movement of the arms, which tends to produce lateral movement of the body.

Mistake #3 The body doesn't roll enough.

Diagnosis Roll is necessary—your torso and legs should roll from side to side to such an extent that your shoulders will alternately point towards the pool bottom.

The problem with arranging all of your sticks (bones) into the correct alignment is that it is very difficult to visualize yourself as you swim. Ask someone knowledgeable, such as a coach or fellow swimmer, to check your body positioning in the water regularly.

The Arm and Hand Stick: The "S" Shaped Curve

You will know it because you will feel it—most swimming power (some experts think nearly all) comes from the arm muscles. If there was only one aspect of swimming on which we could focus, it would have to be the action of the arm stick.

The arm is made up of the following sticks and hinges: the shoulder joint, the upper arm, the elbow joint, the lower arm, the wrist joint, and the hand. Each of these must be coordinated to maximize propulsion.

When your hand first breaks into the water, thumb first, it moves forward to near-full extension. In sequence: the wrist turns; the hand presses out and downward, then scoops inward; the elbow stays high and bends, as the hand draws an "S" shaped curve as it moves under the body. Then, with the elbow at a right angle, the hand pushes straight backward and your pulling arm accelerates quickly. Near the end of the pull phase your elbow extends from the 90 degree position. You are now at the center of the "S" shaped curve that your hand is drawing.

Push your hand back, not out or up, until your elbow is fully extended. As the thumb passes parallel to the thigh, the hand starts upward and breaks the water's surface with the smallest fingers first. Simultaneously, the opposite hand breaks the water's surface in front of your face and begins the "S" shaped curve.

Here are some pointers:

The S-Shaped Curve

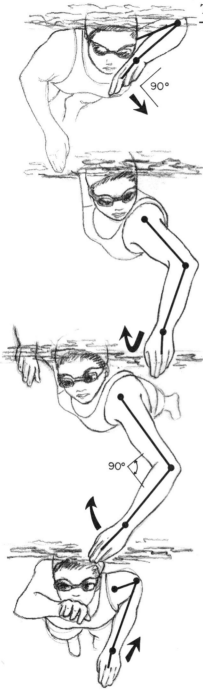

- During the first part of the stroke, the elbow should be higher than the hand.

- The arms are in a continuous alternation, with one arm pulling while the other recovers; there is no pause or rest phase.

- During arm recovery (the time that the arm is out of the water) the elbow initially leads the way, and your hand only passes the elbow once the hand has reached the shoulder point.

- As you pull, imagine reaching over a barrel—that's how it should feel.

The Leg Stick: The Two-Beat Flutter Kick

The primary purposes of the legs during the flutter kick are stability first and forward motion second, since the legs offer very little propulsive force while you are swimming. The stick and hinge sequence is as follows: the hip joint, the upper leg, the knee joint, the lower leg, the ankle joint, the foot.

The leg stick action consists of two upbeats and two downbeats per arm cycle. Since these two directions—up and down—are perpendicular to your direction of travel, it may seem almost counterproductive to kick. It's not. The flutter kick is a very important aspect of the crawl.

It is vital to note that the up-and-down leg movement must not be rigid, or it will cancel itself out. This is one of the reasons why swimmers are flexible—they must have a large range of motion, particularly of the feet and ankles, to allow for forward propulsion, because the feet serve as flippers.

The legs contribute to streamlining and body positioning (alignment) and especially help keep the body from falling prey to the problem of lateral weaving. To be stable, you must flex your hip and push downward with your thigh as you begin the downbeat, and point your toes upward and backward. Because the body rolls as you kick, there is a slight kick outward as well. Your downbeat is finished when the leg is completely straight and just below your body.

The upbeat is a rebound-like action. When the leg is fully extended, you sweep it up, passing the downbeat of the opposite leg. One of the most common mistakes new swimmers make is bending their knees during the upbeat. Keep your knee extended, and it will prevent drag. With the upbeat, as the leg goes toward the surface, use the hip flexors with a relaxed lower leg and ankle.

Here are some pointers:

- The leg action is loose and whiplike, especially the ankles.
- The downbeat is a more powerful action than the upbeat.
- A good toe point is essential to get power from the flutter kick.
- Don't kick too hard—instead use your kick as a rudder.
- Kick only the minimum amount necessary to maintain body positioning.
- The legs hesitate between kicks.

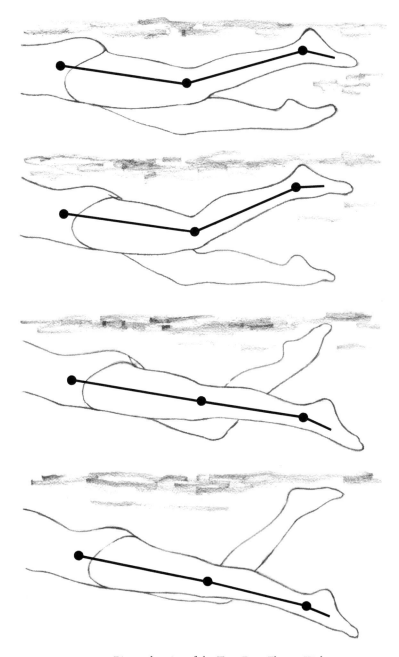

Biomechanics of the Two-Beat Flutter Kick

Swim Equipment

Whether your equipment serves as the tools of your trade or the toys of your sport, it can make a formidable list when you add up all of the accessories that go with racing and training. Keep in mind, though, that everything with the exception of the suit and goggles can be considered optional to some extent.

Swim Fins
Used as a training aid, swim fins can increase the flexibility of your ankles, build the strength of your quadriceps (thigh muscles), and provide a tougher workout by increasing your cardiovascular load.

Hand Paddles
These are usually flat pieces of thin plastic, with surgical tubing attached in order to secure your hands to the paddle. They are used as training devices to improve your armstroke by forcing your hands and arms into the correct stroking pattern. Paddles also increase stroke force, but some research shows that with overuse they may cause shoulder tendonitis.

Pull Buoys
Usually cylindrical pieces of styrofoam, pull buoys allow you to rest your legs by floating them in a natural position, as you isolate your upper body during area-specific workouts. Pulling drills can also be conducted by using small black inner tubes, called "pulling tubes," around your ankles. They provide greater resistance in training than do pull buoys.

Kickboards
Usually made from styrofoam-like materials, kickboards are used to condition your legs and improve the biomechanics of your kick. Kickboards are held with your hands and arms, allowing them to rest, as you isolate the leg movement.

Pace Clock
This is a large clock with sweep second hands; it is used for timing your repeats and determining your departure times. Pace clocks are usually mounted on the wall or seated on the pool deck.

Lycra Speedsuit

These suits are standard racing apparel for competitive triathletes. The lycra stretch fabric adheres tightly to the skin, preventing drag, as well as providing some breast and stomach support. There are different cuts and styles—some even have padded crotches which are useful on the bike and run stages of a triathlon. The suits dry quickly and should last one to two years without stretching out and losing their shape.

Swim Goggles

Though they improve vision, the main purpose for swim goggles is to reduce eye irritation. Cheap or ill-kept ones can be irritating—they may fog frequently, leak, or slip off the face. It's best to buy expensive goggles and eliminate the hassles. Most goggles require numerous adjustments until they fit; it may take a week to get them correctly adjusted.

Defogging Solutions

Swim goggles fog easily, but this can be prevented in a number of ways. You can put either a commercial defogging solution or saliva on them, or buy anti-fog goggles, which are also available.

Heart Rate Monitor

Though expensive (a good one sells for $125+), this device provides an accurate way to measure your pulse. Some can even store times for each segment of your workout ("splits"), so that you can time your repeats and, at the end of the set, replay your exact splits.

Wetsuit

For safety and time savings, a wetsuit has become standard racing gear for triathletes. Wetsuits provide you with extra buoyancy and less drag, so you swim faster and stay warmer. Choose a wetsuit designed specifically for swimming, not waterskiing, windsurfing, or diving.

Swim Training

Swimming uses a different training system, one based on high volume and intensity, from those of cycling and running.

Swimmers follow the interval training system: a method of using multiple, timed, repeat swims, in a combination of rest and work. An example of the interval training system is to swim five 100-yard swim repeats at 80 percent effort, with 30 seconds of rest between each repeat swim. This interval set of repeats is written as follows:

$$5 \text{ x } 100 \text{ yd } / 30 \text{ sec } @ 80\%$$

Parts to the interval: **(N)**   **(D)**   **(R)**   **(I)**

An acronym for this format of swim intervals, and a way to help trigger your memory of the four parts to a set, is "RIND," which stands for rest, intensity, number, and distance. A RIND such as that of an orange or apple is the shell that encases something— in this case it is the shell that encases the interval training system.

All sets contain a RIND, as follows:

R = the rest interval between each repeat (in our example, R= 30 sec.)

I = the intensity of each repeat (in this example, I=80%)
Some swim coaches like to express intensity in other terms such as:
- A specific heart rate like 150-160 beats/minute
- A specific departure time from the wall, such as at every 1 minute
- A perceived exertion rate, such as 7 on a scale of 10

N = the number of repeats in the set (in the above example, N = five repeats)

D = the distance of each of the repeats (in our example, D = 100 yards)

Keep in mind that though most pools are still measured in yards, some are measured in meters, and since triathlon race distances are generally in metric terms, you'll need to be prepared to make the distance conversions. For that purpose, 1 yard=.91 meters, and 1 meter=1.09 yards.

When you design your swim workout, you will be varying your RIND, the four parts to the interval training system. Here are some suggestions on how to build and vary your swim workouts:

(N) The Number of Repeats: A group of interval repeats is called a "set." Each set should last no less and not much more than 10 minutes in total swim and rest time. Ten minutes is the minimum amount of time for a set, because it takes about three to four minutes for your body to warm up to training intensity. The balance of the time is then devoted to stressing the body's cardiorespiratory system so that the "training effect" can occur. The training effect is the improvement to the entire physiological system that occurs as a result of exercise, which enhances your overall athletic performance, no matter the sport.

(**D**) The Distance of Each Repeat: The training effect is not as dependent on the distance of each repeat as it is on the length of time of the entire set. So, to offset boredom, vary your repeats using distances from 25 meters up to several hundred. In a short-course pool, that is, one that is 25 meters in length, a 50-meter repeat will obviously require you to swim continuously for two lengths, whereas in a long-course (50-meter) pool, a 50-meter repeat will only require you to swim one length.

(**R**) Rest Interval between Each Repeat: Rest intervals are usually described as a ratio between the amount of time spent swimming and the amount of time spent resting. Hence, a 5:1 ratio means five minutes of swimming and one minute of resting. The rule of thumb is to keep the rest interval less than one-half the time of the swim, or no more than a 2:1 ratio. The most common ratios are 3:1 or 4:1. This means that if you swim a repeat of 100 yards in 45 seconds, a 3:1 ratio will entail a 15-second rest. Typically, the short rest periods improve aerobic fitness more effectively than the longer ones. Here are some suggested rest intervals based upon the distance of the repeat:

Optimum Rest Intervals for Repeat Swim Distances

Distance	Rest Interval
25 yards/meters	5-10 seconds
50 yards/meters	10-20 seconds
75-100 yards/meters	10-45 seconds
150-200 yards/meters	20-60 seconds
200-400 yards/meters	45 seconds-2 minutes
400 yards/meters and longer	1-3 minutes

(**I**) The Intensity of Each Interval: The best method of maintaining an accurate amount of intensity is by using heart rate as your measuring scale. Since taking your pulse after each interval simply isn't practical, I urge you to use one of the commercial heart rate monitors for swimmers that are available. Most swimmers, though, rely on their subjective perceptions of how hard they are swimming and periodically check their heart rate manually.

If you can join a swim group, do so. They are motivating, social, and, hopefully, the coach can provide you with biomechanical advice. Using rest intervals usually doesn't work with groups, however, there are generally multiple swimmers in a lane, and some are ready to start while others are resting. Therefore, in this situation swimmers use "departure time," rather than rest intervals.

A departure time is the sum of the rest interval and swim interval times. In our example, the departure time equals the rest interval, 30 seconds, plus the length of time it takes you to swim 50 yards—let's say 45 seconds. So, you would add 30 seconds and 45 seconds, and your departure time would equal 1 minute and 15 seconds. You would then depart from the wall for each repeat at the 1 minute and 15 second (1:15) point, as indicated by the pace clock. Some coaches would write this set as follows: 5 x 100 yds @ 1:15.

As your conditioning improves, your departure times will drop. After several weeks it may surprise you, because for the same perceived effort, you will be able to use a 1 minute and 10 second departure time and feel that the workload is the same. This is the training effect—you'll become stronger and fitter and faster.

A powerful swimmer briefly looking up to "sight."

3

The Basic Moves—Bicycling

Bike Biomechanics

In the bike world, the biomechanic's buzzwords are "handling skills," the riding techniques that involve one's ability to control a bike effectively and efficiently. Before you can begin to practice handling skills though, you must have a bike frame that fits your body's frame. If you don't match frames, you will never achieve effective bike handling skills.

According to Elaine Mariolle, co-author of The Woman Cyclist and 1986 Race Across America winner, "You can spend a lot of money and buy the best possible bike, with a custom frame and the finest components, but if it doesn't fit you, you are likely to be miserable."

Really, it's more than likely—you *will* be miserable.

Fitting a Bike

Don't take the usual advice, "Just go to the shop, and they can look at you and tell you what size bike to buy." All you know about that salesperson sizing you up is that they get paid to do it; you don't know if they actually have any expertise.

Take this advice instead—get measured. There are two good measurement methods available today. The first is called the Fit Kit and is available in most quality bike and triathlon stores. A good store should apply the Fit Kit cost against the purchase price of the bike if you ask ahead of time. It takes about 30 minutes and you will be given a complete written set of measurements of what fits your individual anatomy: the saddle height, frame size, crank length, handlebar stem length, and much more.

The second is the Pro Bike Fit, a computerized system that, when given your measurements, will recommend a frame and components to fit your body.

Next, test ride several different bikes that are the right frame size. You may notice that some aren't completely comfortable. That is because most bikes are designed for men's anatomies, not for the size and shape of women's bodies.

Anatomical Differences: Women Compared to Men

As a general rule, there are more similarities than differences between the female and male bodies, but there are some notable differences, not all of which are connected to our various reproductive duties.

At full physical maturity, average females weigh 25 pounds less than average males. In general, a fit body of either sex has a wedge shape: women with wider hips than shoulders, men with wider shoulders than hips. When fat-not-fit, this wedge shape spreads: men become apple-shaped and wide around the midsection, and women become more pear-shaped, storing their fatty tissue in their hips.

In overall anatomical appearance, women are less rugged—their bones are less long, thick, and dense, and their joints are smaller. Other specific anatomical differences for comparable body frames are as follows:

- Men have broader chest circumferences than women.
- Women have narrower shoulder widths than men.
- Women have a larger abdomen, men have a larger thorax.
- The lower leg length of the female is relatively shorter (51.2% of their height) than the lower leg length of the male (52% of their height).
- Men's feet and hands are longer and wider than are women's.
- Males have longer arms, particularly forearms, than females.

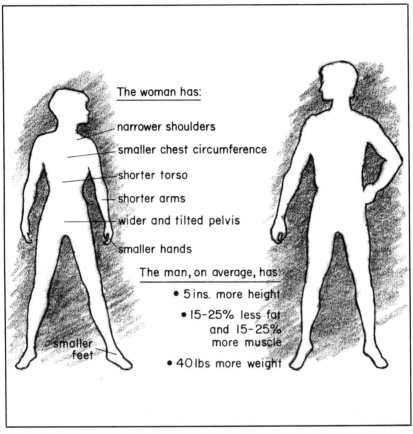

The woman has:

narrower shoulders

smaller chest circumference

shorter torso

shorter arms

wider and tilted pelvis

smaller hands

The man, on average, has:

• 5 ins. more height

• 15-25% less fat
  and 15-25%
  more muscle

• 40 lbs more weight

smaller feet

Notable Differences in Shape and Size between Women and Men

- The pelvis in women is wider than in men.
- The angle of pelvic inclination (pelvic tilt) is greater for women.

If you take the overall measurements of the adult female and compare them with the adult male, there is a sizeable difference. On the average, the male's body measurements are about 108 percent of the body measurements of the female, a size superiority of almost 10 percent.

Interestingly enough, the performance differences (as measured by world records in various sports) are roughly equivalent to the anatomical ones—there is about a 10 percent difference in performance overall. Take a look at the following chart, and you will see what I mean.

WORLD RECORD DIFFERENCES

Running	Women	Men	Percentage Difference
100 meters	10.79	9.93	8.0%
1 mile	4:17:04	3:47:33	11.6%
10 k	31:35:02	27:22	13.3%
26.2 miles	2:22:43	2:08:13	10.2%
			10.78% average

Swimming			
100 meters	54.79	49.36	9.1%
400 meters	4:06:28	3:48:32	7.1%
800 meters	8:24:62	7:52:33	6.3%
1500 meters	16:04:49	14:54:75	7.2%
			7.4% average

Anatomical Differences and Bike Fit

Obviously, anatomical differences affect how bikes fit the human frame. If bikes were fit by height alone, there would be no need for different frame sizes. But bikes are divided into two separately measured units by the seat, which must be fitted to two different parts of the human body: the upper body or torso, and the lower body or leg. The two measurements—torso and leg length—are very different between women and men, and these differences necessitate modifications in bike design.

Georgeanna Terry, whose company, Terry Bicycles, is the only manufacturer that builds bikes solely for women, has taken account of these differences in her production requirements, as shown in the diagram on the following page.

There are other changes in the bike and its components that will facilitate a better match between a woman's frame and a bike. These include: narrower handlebars, shorter stems, shorter crank arms, smaller brake levers, and smaller toe clips. Other manufacturers (Bridgestone, Centurion, Fisher Mountain Bikes, and Univega, among others) have responded to the demand from female cyclists and are producing female-fitted frames as well.

For some help in determining the right-size bike, without using a commercial fitting method, the following chart designed by Elaine Mariolle might be helpful:

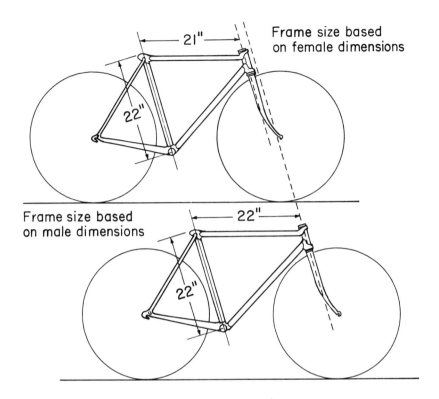

Chart for Sizing a Woman To A Bike

Your Height	Seat Tube Length*	Straddle Height**	Top Tube Length***
Shorter than 4'11"	16	26.1	18.9
4'11" to 5'1"	17	27.3	19
5'1" to 5'3"	18.5	28.7	19
5'3 to 5'4"	20	30.3	19.5-21
5'4 to 5'7"	21.5	31.8	21
Taller than 5'7"	23	33.2	21.5

Reprinted with permission.

These measurements are all in inches. Please note that since many bicycles are measured in centimeters, a metric conversion might have to be made at some point.

*Seat Tube Length: The length from the point where the seat meets the frame to the bottom bracket (the cylinder in which the crank axle rotates).

**Straddle Height: The vertical height from the ground to the top of the top tube.

***Top Tube Length: The length from the seat lug to the head tube lug (the joint between the top tube and the head tube).

In selecting a frame, you are essentially buying two trian-gles that are linked by one common tube, the seat tube. Bikes are measured by the length of the seat tube, not the height of the bike, with common lengths of 19, 21, 23, or 25 inches (some are measured in centimeters).

If a bike isn't available in the exact size that you need, always take the smaller choice. Don't buy one that is the wrong size just because you like the color or because it's all that's avail-able—it's worth it to wait.

You must also keep in mind the differences among vari-ous styles of bikes. For example, the basic difference between a racing bike and a tourer is that the wheelbase (the distance between the front and rear axles) is shorter on the racing bike and the frame angles are steeper. Today's triathlon bikes are unique in their geometry and components—everything from the new design of aero-bars (handlebars), to the smaller (24") front wheels of some time-trial bikes, to Seat Shifters (which shift your seat into different forward and back positions)—are designed for improved efficiency, aerodynamics, and speed.

Now that you know some of the basics of bikes, here's the biomechanics of riding and handling them.

Bike Training—Technique

Once you've become acquainted with your second self, your bike, it's time to introduce the handling skills which will get you where you want to go.

If it's your first time on the bike, it's a good idea to find a quiet street or parking lot to practice. The first biking technique to master (remembering to always wear your bike cleats while training, in order to get used to their feel) is the foot-to-the-ped-al action. If you have toe clips, turn the crank so that the free pedal is in the 1 o'clock position. Tap the back edge of the pedal with your toe, turning the pedal to the upright position, and slide your foot into the cage. The position is awkward at first, but, once you are in and have tightened the toe strap, you will be snugly joined to your bike. You will eventually do the same with your other pedal, but for now leave one foot loose for emergency stops, until you gain your confidence.

If you ride with clipless or step-in pedals, the process is a lot easier. Again, place the pedal upright, in the lowest (6 o'clock) position, step into the clip with your heel high and toe pointed down, then push down firmly with your heel and snap

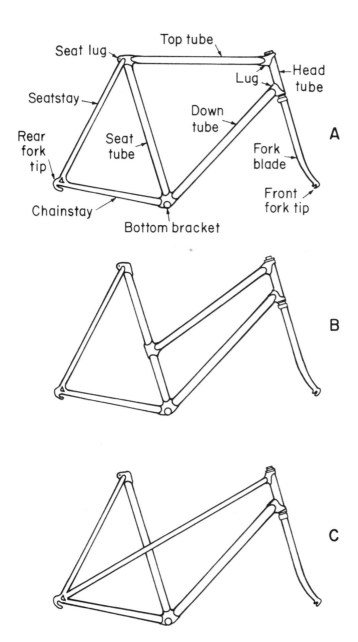

The three frames shown here are: (A) a men's, or diamond, frame; (B) a women's, or dropped, frame with no top tube; and (C) a mixy frame where a tube or pair of tubes runs from the head tube to the rear axle dropouts.

yourself in, as with a ski boot. To release, rotate your foot and pedal to a position parallel to the ground and kick your heel out forcefully, using the toe as a pivot point.

You're now ready to go. Don't be surprised, though, if you go down or crash at some point. A fall is one of the experiences that happen to every rider. In order to minimize your chances of a crash, here are some tips on how to ride more efficiently and safely over a variety of conditions. Follow them.

Riding a Straight Line

This is the first technique you need to learn, and it's the one, if you race, that might keep you from crashing. Other cyclists assume that, once started, you will continue to ride in a straight line without changing direction by even a few inches. That assumption is critical for you to appreciate, because if you

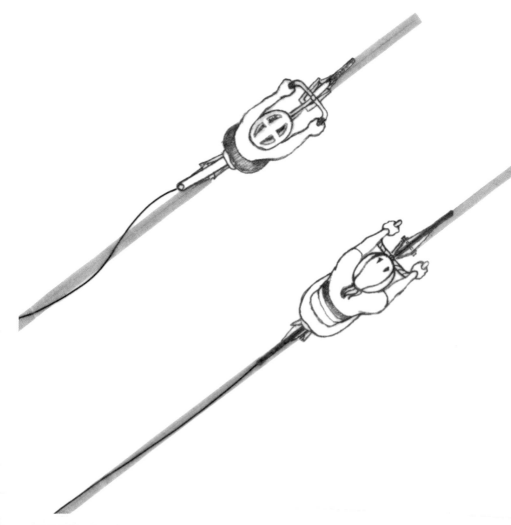

are going to change direction, you *must* let the riders around you know.

Practice riding a straight line by actually riding on a line on a bike trail or parking lot. If you weave extensively, then it could be because your bike doesn't fit you, you have a bent frame or fork, or because you simply need more time in the saddle.

Cornering

To turn or "corner," lean. Unless you are going extremely slow, all your turns will be based on leaning into the turn, not turning the handlebars. Always raise the inside pedal in a turn, so that it doesn't scrape the ground, which may also keep you from a crash. Survey your turn in advance, and pick a line (the path you will take) in the turn. Again, throughout the turn, hold your line.

Stopping

When you stop, always release your right foot from the pedal in advance. There is an obvious safety reason for releasing the right and not the left foot—if you do fall, you will then fall to the right, away from the car lane. Slide off the saddle (seat) just as you come to a complete stop.

The dangers of using your front brakes to stop are mainly mythical—you won't go flying over your handlebars unless you hit your front brakes so hard that you nearly lock them. About 90 percent of your braking power comes from your front brakes, so use them. It's best to use both brakes in tandem, especially if you have to stop quickly. In the rain or on fast downhills, you should pump your brakes just as you would those of your car. Finally, for a slight reduction in speed, usually when you are riding closely behind another rider, "feather" your brakes by squeezing the brake levers slightly.

Spinning

This is a technique of pedaling rapidly (at a high number of revolutions per minute—"rpm") in low gears. The low gears are the easy ones to pedal and the high gears are the difficult ones. Spinning allows you to work more efficiently, by increasing your speed while decreasing the workload. It's like lifting

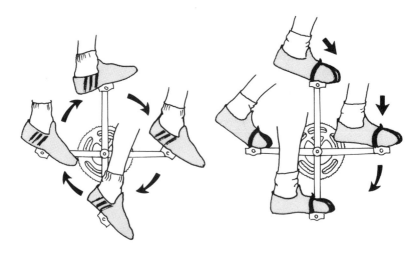

Spinning versus pushing pedaling motion

weights—it's easier to life a light, one-pound weight a hundred times, than a fifty-pound weight twice.

For long-distance riding, most cyclists spin at a pedal cadence (the number of rotations or the rate that you spin) between 75-85 rpm, although there are some who prefer to spin at a cadence of up to 100+ rpm.

If you don't have a cyclometer (also called a bike computer, it is a device that measures speed, cadence, and other important bicycling statistics), then you will have to count your pedal cadence. Count the number of rpm over a 60-second period to find your spin rate. As you learn to spin, start by using extremely low gears and low resistance (ride on a flat course). If you train in low gears on the flats, you may be embarrassed at how slow you actually travel, but you'll get the technique right.

Spinning is one of those techniques that can take a beginner as little as an hour to learn. However, if you already know how to ride, it may take you much longer, since breaking old habits, like braking a heavy vehicle, takes time.

Gears and Shifting

Most racing bikes have 10 speeds, while tourers usually have 15. You can identify a 10 speed bike because it has two front gears called chainrings, and five rear gears, which are the

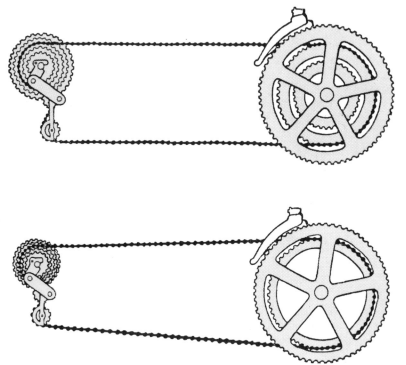

Diagram showing the differences between the touring and racing drive trains. The touring drive train, (A) has wide-range triple front chainwheels, a 14–34-tooth rear freewheel and a long-reach derailleur. The racing drive train, (B) has double chainwheels of just a few teeth difference, a 13–17-tooth rear freewheel and a small-capacity derailleur.

freewheel or rear cluster or rear cog. Fifteen-speed bikes have three chainrings.

When you are in the larger chainring, you have five gear choices, and when you are in the smaller chainring you have another five gear choices, which combine to make ten speeds. The front and rear derailleurs (gear changers) shift the chain from one chainring to another and from one freewheel to another. The lowest gear, the one that is easiest to pedal, is a combination of the smallest front chainring and the largest rear freewheel. The highest gear is just the opposite—the biggest front chainring and the smallest rear cog are joined.

The chainrings and rear clustrers have teeth which may vary in number. The chainrings usually have 52 teeth on the larger and 42 teeth on the smaller gear. A "straight cluster" has a consecutive number of teeth on each gear, such as 13-14-15-16-

17, which is appropriate for flat terrain. Other clusters have a variety of teeth combinations, such as 13-15-17-19-23. When you buy a bike, a good triathlon or bike store will replace the factory freewheel with one that will be best-suited for your needs, depending on the type of terrain on which you ride.

Shifting is easy and should be, when executed correctly, a quiet maneuver. To shift, ease up slightly on your cadence (but don't stop pedaling) and move your gear shift lever forward or back. Click shifting componentry is preset for exactly the place that you want to move the gear shift lever. So, if you hear a rattling noise when you shift, you haven't shifted to exactly the right position. Make a slight adjustment of the lever, maybe an eighth of an inch, and you'll be where you need to be.

Drafting

Riding with a pack of cyclists requires fine-tuned handling skills. If you weave to miss a hole or dodge an object, you may veer into other cyclists and crash. When you attend your first group ride, hang back and learn, because when you are ready to ride in front, you will be responsible for letting the others know what is ahead. Some groups rely on hand signals for turns, potholes, slowing, stopping, and announcing an approaching car, while other groups are more vocal.

It's never a mistake when you pass another rider to always announce (actually shout) these words, "Passing on your right (or left)." The rider whom you are passing probably doesn't know that you are nearby, but they need to know your position in order to ride safely. Also, if a car is coming from behind and you are at the back of the group, yell loudly to the front of the group, "car back," to let everyone know of the car's position. Likewise, if you are in the front and a car is approaching, yell, "car up."

When you ride in packs, you "draft." Drafting is a technique of riding closely behind another cyclist, in their slipstream. This allows the front rider to break the wind for you, so you can sit behind them and ride more easily. Riding the draft can save you about 15 to 20 percent of the energy requirements of riding solo.

Drafting, for fairly obvious reason, is not allowed in triathlons. However, in training you will probably ride with a group, so you'll need to know the skill. First, make sure that it's alright for you to draft—some riders don't want you "on their wheel." The way to ask is to say, "May I sit in?" If you don't ask, you can create a lot of anger.

As you ride in a draft position, you must be extremely focused, because the concentration and skill needed to ride 6 inches to 2 feet behind the rear wheel of another cyclist is intense. When there are several riders drafting, the line of riders is called an echelon or paceline, and the rider in front "pulls"

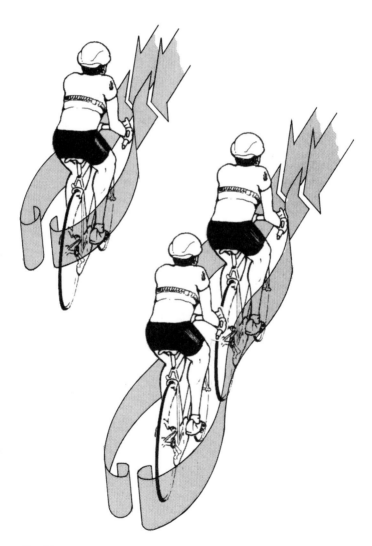

Drafting can save 15–20 percent of the following rider's energy.

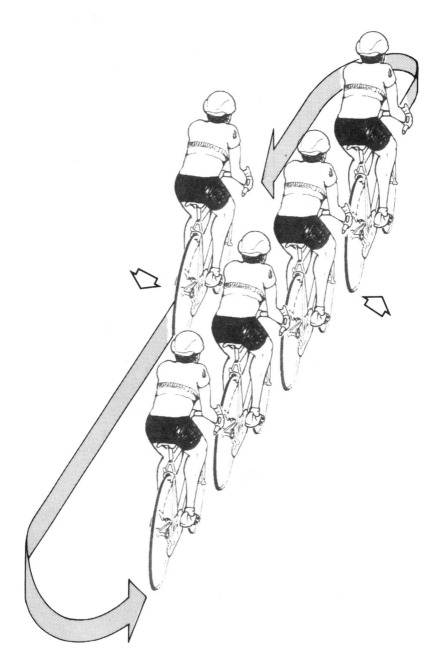

When swinging off, pull to the left, ease off while the paceline passes, tuck in behind the last rider, then accelerate to speed with one or two pedal strokes.

those behind. After her pull, she rotates to the back of the pace-line, and the next rider in line takes the front position and pulls.

When it's your turn to pull, if you can't hold the speed of the paceline, drop back with the leader—it's ok to "sit in the pack" when you are new—all riders have experienced this at one time. Just explain that you are a novice; the others will appreciate the information and encourage you to sit in.

Drafting can be dangerous. Last summer when I was riding with a group, we had a strong side wind, coming from our right. An experienced and powerful rider was in the lead, taking us out at about 23 mph. After taking her two-minute pull, she dropped off to the left. Due to the strong wind, the proper drafting position was about one foot back and two feet to the left, directly in the path of her retreat. As she slowed, we "crossed front wheels," which means her rear wheel struck my front wheel. The rider in the back always goes down in these instances, and I was no exception. I went down hard, hit my head, rolled onto my face, then shoulder, then hip. The next two riders dodged me and stayed upright.

Knocked unconscious, I awoke to find an ambulance crew loading me into their rescue vehicle and dashing me off to the nearest hospital. A concussion, contusions, and a separated shoulder set my training back a few months, but it was a lesson I won't need to repeat and one I don't want you to experience. Drafting can be dangerous.

Climbing

This may seem hard to believe, but experienced cyclists have a passion for climbing hills. Hills are a measure of cyclists' resolve; they present a personalized challenge, and they allow group riders to break up into smaller packs. If you can develop this passion, you will definitely get strong faster.

The easiest way to climb a hill is to start slowly. If it's a short hill, you can bully your way to the top. But if it's a long hill, shift down at the bottom and spin your way to the top. You should try to hold the same cadence you maintained on the flats, but some hills are just too steep or too long, and you will have to ease down to a 40-65 rpm pedal cadence. If you are forced to shift while climbing, try to do it easily and smoothly. First, take the tension off the chain by pedaling as lightly as pos-sible and then shift, but not too quickly—you don't want to get your chain jammed into the freewheel.

Practice riding hills. Find a hill that is challenging and work it—do repeat rides up the hill. As you gain strength and confidence, you can try steeper hills and train on them for your repeats.

Your breathing technique on hills is important. My first year of racing triathlons in Europe, a Frenchman rode up next to me and tried to start a conversation. My high school French just didn't make casual chit-chat possible, and I really didn't want to carry on a conversation during a race, when I was using all my oxygen for more important matters. Curiously, he started breathing slower and deeper and gestured as if to demonstrate this to me. I realized then that I was breathing quickly and from the top of my lungs and that he was trying to teach me the correct way to breathe on the uphills. So I tried it—taking deep breaths, with my stomach cavity pushing out as I breathed in. Try it yourself—it works.

As you reach the summit of a hill, keep pedaling. Upshift as you descend and maintain your cadence on the downhill, until you hit the point when you can gain more speed by holding a tightly tucked position than by pedaling. Lower yourself into the tucked position early on the downhill. In the tucked position, your chest is lowered to the handlebars, your knees firmly clutch the top tube, and your elbows are pointed in, with your head lowered.

Climbing out of the Saddle

There are two different times that cyclists climb out of their saddles:

- Racers use this technique to jump ahead of the pack or to break away.
- Riders use this technique to power up hills.

To do either, you shift into your middle gears and then stand up onto your pedals. Grasp the brake lever posts or, if you have aero-bars, put both your hands on the handlebars, each about three inches away from the stem. Using your arms to pull up on the bars, lean your bike alternately left and right at about a 20 degree tilt, over whichever leg is exerting force at any given point. Your leg should be directly over the pedal in this position, which will give you extra power, and the wheels will still track a straight line. Slow your cadence and work the hill, breathing deeply and with control, so that you rhythmically

When climbing a hill out of the saddle, you angle your body over the pedals, with your hands gripping the brake-lever hoods.

match cadence and breath. Use climbing out of the saddle on hills as a relief from the grind of sitting in a low gear and slowly working your way to the top, and take advantage of your position to stretch your back.

To win races over uneven terrain, champion cyclists use a combination of both climbing methods, climbing both in and out of the saddle. Remember, standing and climbing will not only break the grind of an uphill, it can also power you away from your competition.

Bike Equipment

There are three pieces of equipment that together make a complete bike: the frame, the components or parts, and the accessories. Since we discussed the frame earlier, we will now take a look at the rest of the picture.

Components

Wheels

All of your energy, sweat, and work are aimed at making your wheels roll, so they can be one of your best bike component investments; the better your wheels are, the faster you go.

Alloy rims both outperform steel rims, especially in wet conditions, and are significantly lighter. A heavy-duty steel rim and tire weigh about 1,300 grams per wheel. An equally strong alloy rim and tire weigh only about 700 grams—that's 2.5 pounds less per pair. By all means, buy the best wheel that you can afford. It's better to ride a $300 bike with quality lightweight wheels, than a $1,000 bike with cheap ones.

Tires

The tubular tire or "sew-up" is a tube sewed into a tire that is then mounted on a wheel rim with glue. A clincher tire, on the other hand, has a lip that secures to the lip of the rim. Tubulars are great for racing, but are extremely difficult to use for training. Since the tube is sewn into the tire, when you get a flat you

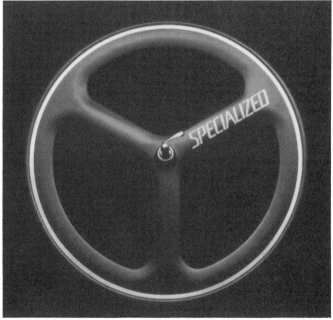

The Specialized composite racing wheel—one of the most advanced cycling products in the world today.

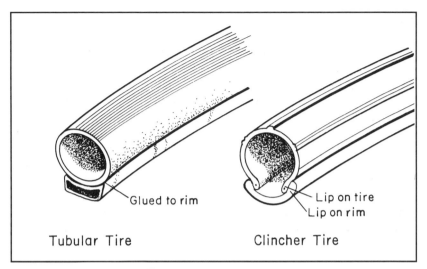

Glued to rim   Lip on tire
                Lip on rim

Tubular Tire   Clincher Tire

Two Different Tire and Rim Cross Sections

must replace the tire and then repair it later, a time consuming and expensive process. Today, there is little weight or performance difference between tubulars and clincher tires, so I recommend choosing clincher tires over tubular ones.

Always buy high-pressure tires rated at 75 pounds per square inch (psi) or more. The higher the pressure, the less the roll resistance, or the mechanical drag, caused by contact with the road and the faster you will go!

Saddles

The difference between pleasure and misery on a bike can often be traced to its seat.

There are far too many saddles on the market to describe. They can be made of leather, plastics, or synthetics, and may come with padding of air, foam, gel, or other materials.

Replace the stock saddle that comes with your bike with a saddle that fits your buttocks. I recommend that you try the saddles specifically designed for a woman's pelvic anatomy— they fit better and are widely available. The companies producing female-fitted seats include Vette, Selle, Avocet, and Italia, among others.

The most important rule for becoming good friends with your saddle is to break it in slowly. You should limit yourself to short rides at first, and allow a long enough break-in period (several hundred miles is best) to adjust to it.

Brakes

Brakes can mean the difference between life and death and should be treated with the utmost respect.

There are two types of caliper brakes: sidepull brakes, where the brake cable enters the brake arms (called calipers) from one side, and centerpulls, which have a transverse cable entering from the middle. Sidepull brakes are preferable.

Make sure that the brake pads ("blocks") are of quality materials and contact the rims squarely. Check the brake levers to see if they fit your hand size, since women usually need smaller brake levers, such as those on a mountain bike. If the bike is equipped with safety levers (they are parallel to and underneath the handlebars), have them removed; they reduce steering control and limit the amount of travel of the main brake lever.

Handlebars and Stem

The standard "drop" handlebars work fine for triathlons. However, if you can upgrade, add a pair of clip-on aerodynamic bars with elbow pads, called "aero bars". You might then want to consider replacing your stem (it's what connects the handlebars to the steering tube and forks) with that of a mountain bike stem, in order to raise your upper body when you are riding on the clip-ons. You should also take advantage of the fact that bike stems are made in varying lengths and get one which best accommodates the length of your upper torso.

Other Components

Shop for quick-release hubs. These allow you to flick a lever and easily remove the wheel from the bike, providing ease in fixing flats and with transportation.

If your bike is so equipped, replace its toe clips, straps, and pedals with clipless pedals. They are safer, faster to step into, and lighter-weight.

Ask to make sure that the frame tubes have reinforced lugs at the joints.

Lastly, look at the crankarms and find out whether or not they are cotterless; it's better that they be so.

Hubs, spokes, rims, bottom brackets, headsets, derailleurs, and all of the other components may also be individually selected. If you choose to assemble a bike in this way, by selecting custom components, you might want to hang them on a custom frame in order to assemble a complete bike. If you wish to go custom all the way, start by purchasing a bike book that discusses custom bikes and study the most recent issues of bicycling magazines. There really are tremendous advantages, especially for women, in putting together a custom bike.

Probably the most important component to hang on your frame is a non-tangible one—the warranty. Parts usually have lifetime warranties, and frames and forks are generally covered for 90 days. A good dealer will offer a 30-day free adjustment or tune-up for your new bike. And you'll want to take advantage of this and have the shop check all of the components to ensure that they are working properly, the cables especially, since they stretch a good deal when they are first used.

Accessories

Helmet

This is the single most important item that you must purchase. In fact, one saved my life this year. After my bike accident (and after I awoke from the concussion), I looked at the two cracks and the skid marks that cut deeply into the side of my helmet, and I was unbelievably thankful, because the helmet had cracked open and not my cranium.

Helmets must meet the safety requirements set by either one of two different industry watchdogs: Snell (the Snell Memorial Foundation) or ANSI (American National Standards Institute). If the helmet meets their rigorous testing, a sticker is attached as a seal of approval. There are three other requirements to take into consideration: fit/comfort, ventilation, and weight. I train using a heavy, more protective helmet made by Etto, and I race in a light, less protective model by Giro.

Some riders take their helmets off during the ride and hang them from the handlebars, and I can't express how stupid I think they are. Helmets are made to wear, not to hang on your bike. My unbreakable rule is that I won't ride with anyone who doesn't wear a helmet—my cycling partners either wear a helmet, or we don't ride together. It's a good rule.

Two Pumps

The first one to purchase is a frame pump, which you will carry with you on your bike, because it's inevitable that you will flat. The second pump should be a high-pressure floor pump with a pressure gauge. You can only pump a bike tire to about 60-80 psi with a frame pump, so you need a floor pump to completely fill your tires to the higher psi required for efficient riding.

Tire Repair Accessories

Buy a bike accessory bag that will fit under your saddle, and at a minimum put in the bag these items: a 25 cent coin (for a pay telephone call), three tire irons and a patch kit, and your personal identification information, including an emergency phone number. You might also consider carrying an air canister (with adaptor), which can function as a quick alternative to hand pumping your tires after a flat.

Cage and Water Bottles

If your bike doesn't come with one, buy either a lightweight alloy or tough-plastic water bottle cage or one of the kind that attaches behind your saddle for ease and aerodynamics. I actually recommend carrying two water bottles for those hot days when you will really need them.

Cyclometers

These tiny computers are a delight, because they give you informational feedback as you ride. A cyclometer attaches to your handlebars and works using magnetic impulses, which are transmitted to a computer chip, from a pick-up device mounted on the wheel. Bike computers measure pedal cadence, speed in miles per hour (or kilometers per hour), average speed, distance traveled (trip distance), total distance traveled to date, time of day, and duration of the ride. Some cyclometers can also display several of these data functions simultaneously.

Heart Rate Monitors

A heart rate monitor has a computer chip that measures your pulse rate and transmits this data to a watch-like device. Some pulse monitors can give you heart rate measurements at specific times or miles and store the information for later retrieval. For years, I have used one when I train seriously, and it is a key component to my racing successes, because I've learned to race according to my pulse readings, not my sense of exertion. I have long used the CIC (Computer Instruments Corporation) heart rate monitors, and they have never failed me.

Locks

You may need one, but I caution you against using them, because no matter how good a lock is, it can be broken. Your only reliable lock is to watch your bike yourself. Still, if you have to leave your bike momentarily, use a lightweight cable lock that can fit in your under-the-saddle bike bag and weave the cable through your wheels.

Reflectives
Any gear that you can acquire which provides reflective properties is a plus. Reflective clothing, equipment, patches, vests, reflectors attached to pedals, and tape for your helmet all light you up in a world where, as a cyclist, you appear obscure not only to cars, but also to runners or other cyclists. Attach a rechargeable nickel-cadmium, battery-powered lamp with halogen bulbs to your frame if you are going to ride at night—the beams are bright enough that you really can see the road.

Remove These Accessories
Stock bikes are frequently equipped with unnecessary accessories. For example, kickstands are heavy and really serve no useful purpose for a cyclist. You also don't need reflectors on your wheels; they slow you down, and, if you are going to ride at night, you will wear reflective gear and use a front and rear light. Nor do you need valve stem caps, those little black plastic caps that screw onto the tire's valve stem. They slow you down when you want to fix a flat and serve no valuable purpose.

Bikewear
Hardcore cyclists are very resistant to change. Most will only wear black shorts, hat helmets, and think aero-bars are for triathlete-geeks, not real cyclists. When technological change indisputably produces an item that out-performs the one they have been using, the hardcore still don't like to accept it or make a change.

The cycling apparel industry has had an extremely difficult time overcoming this phenomenon. Getting even a small percentage of cycling consumers to wear high-visibility apparel for safety and colorful designs for fun and fashion, and getting them to understand that shorts with leather-padded crotches cause more problems than they solve, has taken a decade.

Triathlon enthusiasts are diametric opposites—offer them something new that outperforms what they have been using, and they buy it by the thousands. Thanks to the purchasing power of triathletes, the cycling industry finally has an incentive to manufacture and market cutting-edge, high-tech, high performance products and apparel.

It's as important to dress in performance wear as it is to invest in performance components and equipment. Researchers have used wind-tunnel tests to measure performance differences among cyclists wearing different types of apparel and have demonstrated that wearing tight-fitting cyclewear can save the rider 10 percent or more in energy costs and time.

Shorts

The two concerns for all apparel are warmth and moisture control, the fabric's ability to wick dry. In the old days (maybe 20 years ago), riders wore black wool shorts with a chamois patch sewn into the crotch. Today, there are new fabrics and methods of construction which have changed all that.

In cold-weather riding, the new polypropolene blends are warmer and wick sweat better than do wools. In hot weather, lycra stretch blends reflect the heat, allow perspiration to evaporate, quick-dry, and contour to the body more comfortably. Thankfully, chamois-lined pads have been replaced with softer and more hygienic polyester pads. Or, you can train comfortably without pads, in lycra fitness or cross-training shorts, instead.

Cycling shorts are worn without underpants, which are generally uncomfortable and annoying while bicycling. Therefore, because of the heat and sweat, cycling shorts must be washed after each ride. If you have problems with yeast infections, try different types of fabric blends in the inner-lining. You will probably need several pairs of shorts if you ride frequently.

Shirts

Anything snug will do in this area. Some women prefer a lycra-bra top with an over-shirt that is removed once they are warmed up. However, if you crash and your shoulders aren't covered, you risk serious abrasions.

In the pre-triathlon era, women wore black wool jerseys (to match the color of bike grease) with pockets sewn onto the back. The term "bike jersey" comes from those olden days, when the shirts were made from wool jersey material. Today, like shorts, cycling jerseys are constructed from performance fabrics and are cut in fashionable styles.

In colder weather, multiple layers of apparel are recommended: a durable wind-jacket (preferably water resistant), over a long-sleeve polypropolene-blended turtleneck, over a polypropolene short-sleeve shirt, over a polypropolene tank makes four layers, and that should be enough to keep you warm in most conditions. If you want more, add arm and leg warmers to your ensemble.

Cross-training apparel is currently being produced by women's activewear companies, such as Danskin and Moving Comfort, as well as by Nike, Hind, and other fine manufacturers. Cross-training apparel is designed for multi-fitness athletes who want to wear the same apparel for cycling, running, cross-country skiing, rock climbing, swimming, and other sports, and is ideal for your tri-training needs.

And, about those pockets sewn on the back of bike jerseys, most triathletes prefer to carry their extra stuff—food, sunscreen, tires—in fanny packs or under-the-seat accessory packs. It's easier to carry your gear in a fanny pack which can be taken off, than to wear everything stuffed into pockets worn on your back.

Gloves

Cycling gloves are cut off at the knuckles for grip-power. They are designed to protect you from the road shock that is transfered to your hands through the handlebars and to protect your hands when you crash. However, I've always preferred to pad my handlebars, not my hands, with Spenco handlebar material and to avoid crashing. This means that I don't wear cycling gloves unless I need them for warmth. It's your choice.

Cleats

Cycling shoes are in a state of change. With the variety of clipless pedals available, you first need to decide on what pedals you want to ride, before you decide on the cleats to fit them. For years, it's been impossible to find comfortable cleats, because they have uniformly been designed on men's (somewhat wider) foot proportions, but today a number of companies are building cleats specifically for women. When you shop, look for lightness in the shoe, stiffness in the sole, and adjustable cleat plates.

After you buy your cleats you must still adjust them to your pedals. For the first several weeks, carry tools with you when you ride, so that you can readily adjust the pedal-to-cleat position. To position the face plate on the cleat sole, ride with the cleats slightly loose—not so loose that they fall off, but not so tight that you can't change them. When you feel the position is right, tighten them. Draw this newly-tightened pattern on the sole and repeat the previous procedures. Once you have drawn the same pattern three times, tighten your cleats for good.

Socks, Hats, and Eyewear
If it's hot, I wear neither a hat under my helmet nor socks. If the weather turns cool, all of that changes. I hate to be cold, so I adopt the attitude that there's no cold weather, only warm clothing.

Investing in quality protective clothing is the key to never being cold. Wearing polypro socks (with plastic baggies over them, if you need to) and bike booties over your shoes is usually enough to keep your feet warm. Placing a hat under your helmet may cause a problem with a good fit, but it does keep your head warm. Plastic-framed glasses or, better still, ski goggles will protect your eyes from both bugs and the elements, and ski masks or balaclava can further cover and warm your face.

Dress for the ocassion
The temperature, the sun exposure, the rain (hopefully not snow), the fog, the wind speed, and the strenuousness of your ride will ultimately determine the ideal mix of clothing for you to wear. Dress for success, and be prepared to strip it off or pile it on as needed.

The Principles of Training

All training systems, no matter the sport, are based on two and only two methods: continuous training and intervals. These two methods are measured by the length in duration, distance, and intensity of a workout bout and are accomplished either continuously or intermittently.

Each of these methods has a different physiological purpose. Intervals are designed to increase power and are associated with anaerobic training, whereas in continuity training, the main purpose is to develop the aerobic side of the fitness equation, endurance.

The concept of aerobics is still not well understood, although it has been bantered about among athletes for 25 years. The grandfather of aerobics, Dr. Ken Cooper, gave a lecture when I was in graduate school in exercise physiology at UC Berkeley, and said, "Aerobic exercises are those that usually involve endurance activities which don't require excessive speed. In fact, when recommending various kinds of aerobic exercise, I always stress that it's better to use long, slow distances [or LSD] than it is to rely on short, fast bursts of energy."

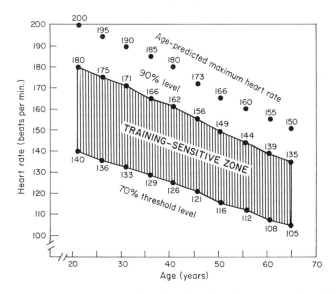

When training, maintain a workload or effort that keeps your pulse within the training zone.

Anaerobic training is exactly the opposite—it's a form of exercising which is so intense that the body is subjected to oxygen deprivation or "debt."

The two types of training—continuous and interval—are sometimes combined. For example, it is quite possible to train continuously, at a constant effort, when bicycling, running, or swimming. However, if the terrain varies or the water current changes, the intensity of your workout will change and an interval factor comes into play. The purpose of combining the two methods is to train both physiological systems—aerobic and anaerobic—during the same workout.

In either method, there are three components, which you can remember by thinking of Nike's "Just Do It" slogan. The three components spell out "D.I.D.," so you can look at your training as if you just "DID" it. "DID" stands for duration, intensity, and distance. The first "D," duration, is how long a training period lasts. The second letter, "I," is for intensity, which is usually measured in heart rates. A lower heart rate, say less than 60 percent of your maximum, means less intensity. Moderate intensity is usually in the 60 to 80 percent range of your adjusted maximum heart rate, and high intensity or sub-anaerobic training is above the 80 percent range. The ideal training heart rate range is between 60 to 90 percent of your adjusted maximum heart rate. The third letter, "D," stands for distance, which is measured in miles (or kilometers) and yards (or meters).

The formula for determining your training heart range is as follows:

1. Figure out your Maximum Heart Rate (MHR) by subtracting your age from 220.

2. Subtract your Resting Heart Rate (RHR) (determine your RHR first thing in the morning before you get out of bed) from your MHR to obtain an adjusted MHR.

3. Multiply the adjusted MHR by the level of intensity percentage.

4. Add your RHR back into the result to find your Training Heart Rate (THR) for the percentage used in step 3.

Here's an example of how to calculate the range of my THR, using my age, 43:

Steps	Low Intensity	Steps	High Intensity
1.	220 - 43 = 177	1.	220 - 43 = 177
2.	177 - 57 = 120	2.	177 - 57 = 120
3.	120 x .60 = 72	3.	120 x .90 = 108
4.	72 + 57 = 129	4.	108 + 57 = 165

So, my THR is between 129 and 165 beats per minute.

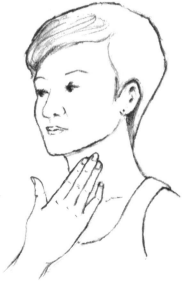

I frequently wear a heart rate monitor when running, cycling, or swimming, which measures and transmits my heart rate to a watch-like device that I wear on my wrist. Visually monitoring its read-out allows me to make sure that I stay within my range.

For those without a fancy machine, you can manually measure your heart rate by taking four fingers of either hand and compressing them against the artery that is just to the side of your trachea (the air tube in your neck). Count your pulse for six seconds and add a zero after that number, and that will give you your heart rate per minute. For example, if you count seven beats in six seconds your pulse is 70 beats per minute.

Bike Training

When I first began entering triathlons, deep inside I still considered myself a runner. At that point, the bike leg of a triathlon was merely an obstacle before the run. Finally, a fellow competitor informed me of my problem, saying, "Sally, you are slow on your bike because you haven't learned to fall in love with it." It was true; I was not particularly strong on the bike for two reasons: I didn't know how to train, and my buttocks were not in love with the bike saddle.

It takes more than mere hours in the saddle to be "bike fit." You can ride comfortably for hours on a bike and gain only the benefits of burning calories and seeing the countryside— that's called exercise, not training. If you are not training, there is no plan, there are no exercise physiology principles being practiced, and there will be little to no improvement.

You can learn to train on the bike by utilizing the same interval principles used in swimming (RIND: rest, intensity, number, distance), blended with the principles of DID training (duration, intensity and distance). Here are some different types of bike workouts that either focus on intervals or on continuous training:

• **Sprints:** A maximum effort for short bursts, followed by easy, spinning rest periods. Using telephone poles, sprint for two poles and rest for three poles, after a long warm-up period. In the beginning, do three to five sets per workout, and vary both quantities of sets and distance (number) of poles.

• **Long Intervals:** These should be two to four minutes in duration, with your heart rate rising close to its maximum. Long intervals are on the border between anaerobic and aerobic training. Using time as your gauge, do a "ladder" of progressively longer intervals with 1:1 rest ratios. The first step up the ladder is two minutes "on" (riding as hard as you can), followed by two minutes "off" (easy spinning for recovery). The next step is three minutes on and three minutes off. The final step up the ladder is four minutes of hard riding, followed by four minutes of rest riding. Next, go down the ladder using the reverse order.

• **Anaerobic Threshold Training:** This is a medium intensity level of training, from four to 30 minutes in length.

Continuously set a speed (using your cyclometer) which is difficult, but not impossible, to maintain for the duration of the
workout. Let's say that you ride your long intervals (2-4 minutes)
at 19 mph. For anaerobic threshold training, you would back
down from this speed to 16-17 mph.

• **LSD:** Long slow distances are relaxed endurance workouts at 65 to 75 percent of your maximum heart rate, for as long
as you want to ride (beyond 30 minutes). You are at aerobic
training levels and the pace is relatively easy.

There are hundreds of other bike training workouts that
you can use in your systematic training schedule. Design them
yourself—it's part of the fun. You can also join bike training
groups and discover what other cyclists find most beneficial.

One of my training partners loves to hammer on the
bike—and to draw me into it. We have a favorite workout that
we have nicknamed the "hawk ride". We'll ride a five-mile
warm-up out into the northern part of the city and head out on
a quiet road which leads towards the airport. I then start by
climbing out of the saddle and powering ahead of Tommy. He
gives me 30 seconds and then starts to chase me down. It takes
him about a minute to catch and pass me; I then stand up on
my pedals again and accelerate to catch his draft. He pulls us
forward until we have reached the end of a three- or four-
minute interval.

One day, a hawk followed us and swooped down on
Tommy. He was so frightened that he must have passed me at
27 mph, as I just couldn't keep up. His best efforts didn't stop
the hawk, though; she continued to tirelessly dive at him for
another several minutes.

When you train systematically, you are to the casual
exerciser what the hawk was to Tommy—a faster, more elegant
and efficient life-form.

4

The Basic Moves—Running

Run Biomechanics

Running is the art of fluid, forward propulsion, driven by the synchronization of all of your body's parts, up to and including the mental one.

Efficient running is based upon economy of motion. When you run economically, like an efficient car you will get more miles per gallon of energy, and your engine will run with fewer breakdowns, as well as less wear and tear.

Imagine yourself replicating each of the following movements. This is the ideal running form, starting from the top and going down:

Head: Your chin is up, and your eyes look forward at least 10 feet, preferably toward the horizon. Breathing is through your mouth, and your jaw and face are so relaxed that they might bounce as you run.

Shoulders: They are relaxed and level to the ground.

Arms: Bent 90 degrees at the elbows (which are within 1 inch of your waist), your arms rotate freely in an arc that projects forward and backward, not rotating around your axis. Your hands should cross your center-line (that imaginary line from your nose, through your navel, to your feet), and the swinging of your arms should allow them to freely cut a course between your hipbone and bust line.

Hands: Your wrists are straight and pointing forward, while your hands are loosely cupped with the thumb and third finger touching (no clenched fists). Your palms should face inward toward each other.

Back: The spine is upright and erect, neither leaning forward nor arching back, but instead it is straight and perpendicular to the ground. If a string were attached to the back of your head, your back would be touching it along its entire length.

Chest: Your chest is lifted up, as if you are being pulled forward by a rope attached to your sternum. Your chest actually leads the way as you run.

Hips: The pelvis is tucked under and your hips are also pushed forward. If you were to put your hands on your buttocks and push them forward, you would feel your shoulders, head, and hips all line up.

Legs: Again, your limbs should be moving in a forward and backward direction, with no rotation around your central axis (the vertical line extending through the center of your body). Keep your feet low to the ground, with little back-kick (unless you are sprinting—sprinters need the power achieved through high knees and long stride lengths). Faster running is accomplished by increases in stride frequency, so the shorter the stride, the more strides you can take and the faster you will go.

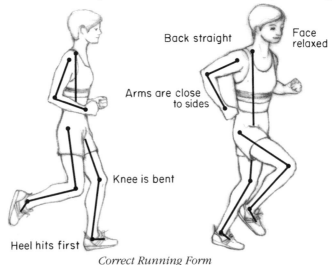

Back straight

Face relaxed

Arms are close to sides

Knee is bent

Heel hits first

Correct Running Form

Feet: Land quietly and softly with little sound on impact, and take care that your stride length is comfortable and not over-extended. Land on your heels first and roll forward off your toes; the only time your toes strike first is if you are sprinting. Your feet should cut a course directly underneath you, not out to the sides.

One of the best ways to check your form is to watch yourself run as you pass the glass windows of store fronts. Hopefully, what you'll see will be the efficient conversion of all energy to forward motion.

The best way to learn to run efficiently is to practice and develop a running style in which all body motion is in a straight, forward direction. There should be no side-to-side action, and gravity should keep you low to the ground.

When you run efficiently, you should feel light and quick—it's a feeling of prancing, not lumbering. Practice breathing deeply (also called "belly breathing"), as your breaths should be full, not shallow or from the top of your lungs.

Changing your running form is like changing your signature—it's something you have to constantly practice. Dedicate one day a week to training in your new efficient form, and work on it so hard that it becomes imprinted as your new signature.

When you have it down, efficient running is like being on cruise control—you can just set the form and the speed and run effortlessly for what seems like forever.

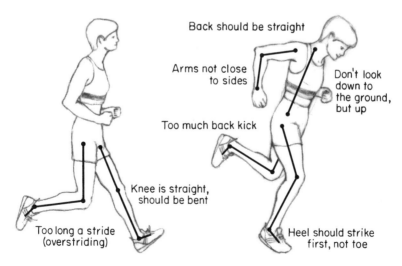

Incorrect Running Forms

Running Equipment

During the past 25 years that I have been competing athletically, there have been two major changes that have driven the footwear and activewear side of sports equipment: the mass participation of women (who sweat and no longer "glow"), and the commitment that women have made to training and not just exercising.

Today, most of us want to have fun as we train, but we also take our sports, training, and equipment seriously.

Shoes

When I first started selling athletic shoes in my *FLEET FEET SPORTS* store in 1976, I ran into two problems: first, there were few styles specifically designed for women's feet, and, second, the ones that were made for men, and the suppliers added the word "lady" before the name—like the Nike "Lady Cortez". Today both these situations have changed. Manufacturers now recognize female athletes as women and have exchanged the term "women" for "lady," and around 90 percent of shoe companies have taken to building women's shoes around the shape of a woman's foot, instead of just producing scaled-down versions of male-shaped ("lasted") shoes.

Running shoes ("flats") are the single most important piece of equipment for a runner. If you have never run in a pair of real running shoes, immediately go to a specialty sports shop and take a pair for a test ride. They are so incredible, compared to cross-trainers or tennis sneakers, that you won't leave the shop without them.

With new styles being released every six months and old styles being discontinued just as quickly, it is impossible to describe training shoes based on model or style. You no longer can find the right shoes and then keep purchasing them over the years—they will probably be discontinued before you wear through your first pair. Rather, to find the right shoes for you, look for a pair that provides shock absorption, stability, adequate flexibility, pronation support (for the way the foot rolls in after contact with the ground), and motion control. The biomechanics of your foot should match perfectly with the structural performance of your running shoe, and only a specialist who knows the current technology in performance footwear can help you with this.

Your basic choice is between racing flats (which weigh about 5 ounces) and training flats (which are about 10-14 ounces). For now, select the heavier but more stable training flats. Later, buy a pair of the racers—they are heavenly and make you feel almost barefoot when you run. If you have a wide foot, you might want to experiment with men's models, so keep in mind that an equivalently sized men's shoe will be 1 1/2 sizes less than a women's shoe (for example, a women's 8 equals a men's 6 1/2). Your new flats do not require a break-in period, just lace them up, put on a pair of lace locks (plastic devices that prevent your laces from coming untied), and take off for an enjoyable few miles.

When you reach the half-life of your running shoes (at roughly 500 to 750 miles or 12 months, whichever comes first), purchase another pair, but of an entirely different technology and style. Then alternate wearing the old pair with the new ones. One of the main reasons for running injuries is wearing the same shoes for every run. If you have a biomechanical weakness and you wear the same pair for every workout, you could fall prey to a cumulative injury effect and be seriously injured.

Maintain your running shoes and don't use them for other sports—these are sport-specific footwear, not cross-training shoes. Occasionally check the wear points on your soles and, if you wear them out, especially in one place, either buy some patching goo from the running/triathlon store or get a new pair—the midsoles are probably shot anyway, as the outsoles should last for a thousand miles, unless you are a foot-dragger.

Another word of advice from an old shoe dog, buy the best pair that you can afford. Choose value over price, because training flats are an investment. It's cheaper to buy top-of-the-line running shoes than it is to pay for one visit to a doctor's office with a foot injury.

Sports Bras

When I first started running, there were no sports bras. Women wore either a Speedo swim suit (interestingly, we still do today) or a support bra. Now there are a half-dozen companies that make sports bras, and no longer are bras uniformly white—they are designed with wild patterns and prints and can even be worn as outer-wear.

Bras that are designed for athletics, rather than aesthetics, serve two primary purposes. First, sports bras prevent a variety of possible injuries to breast tissue: contusions, soreness or abrasions such as jogger's nipple (raw and/or bleeding nipples due

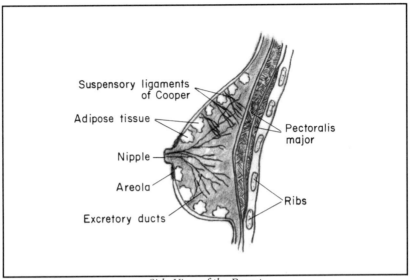

Suspensory ligaments of Cooper

Adipose tissue

Pectoralis major

Nipple

Areola

Ribs

Excretory ducts

Side View of the Breast

to prolonged rubbing against a bra or shirt), or hematomas. Secondly, sports bras provide support to breast tissues from excessive movement.

Proper bra fit is the key to preventing breast movement during vigorous activity. The bra should limit the movement of the breast in reference to the body, allowing it only to move with the trunk, rather than bouncing separately. Accordingly, athletic bras should provide you with the following benefits:

- wide straps that are non-elastic and designed not to slip off the shoulders, such as the Y-back design;
- covered fasteners that do not cause abrasions;
- a nonmetal underwire, such as a wide cloth band, that prevents the bra from riding up over the breasts;
- construction from absorptive, nonallergenic, and nonabrasive materials with little elasticity, such as the "Cool-Max" fabrics;
- good upward support;
- limited motion of the breasts in relationship to the movement of the body;
- distribution of the weight of the breasts evenly over the rib cage and the back, rather than on the shoulders.

Try on several different styles and test them by jumping up and down and by swinging your arms, both over your head and in running-style. Also take a few deep breaths, as a bra

With three miles to the finish of the Ironman, Ironwoman Sally Edwards wearing a trisuit and a smile, knows that in every race there is a moment to smile.

should not interfere with breathing; a sports bra should be firm, but not tight or restrictive to motion.

Apparel

In her 20-year-old, best-selling classic, "Women's Running," Joan Ullyot wrote, "Apart from shoes, what you choose to wear is unimportant." At that time, most of us would have agreed with her, but her statement just isn't true in the 1990s. It's not that you have to dress for success, but rather it's that performance apparel can make a performance difference. Apparel that fits and is of the right fabric can prevent chafing, wick the perspiration away from your body, maintain warmth, lower wind resistance, and prevent drag in the water and through the air. For any one of those features alone, it's worth it to be choosy.

Bottoms

You have a lot of choices. First, fitness or "compression" shorts are made of stretch fabrics and are slightly longer than normal shorts, usually extending to just above the knee (which may prevent thigh chafing). Tights are full length, with stirrups, zippers, or neither, and are great for cold weather. Tricot nylon shorts, with liners cut to a woman's body shape, are lightweight (actually, it feels like you have nothing on) and durable. Briefs or "butt huggers" might work for elite runners, though they leave little to the imagination, but not for me.

Tops
The layered approach in apparel works for both its insulating properties and convenience. In cold weather, layering starts with a sports bra (always, for me), then continues with a polypropolene-blend, short-sleeve top, a long-sleeve shirt and a jacket or vest that is both warm and breaks the wind. All else you will need is to add a few turtlenecks to your wardrobe, and you'll have your top covered.

Tri-suits
These one-piece outfits are a combination of a fitness short and a swimsuit top, merged together in a lycra-blended fabric. They are sleek and true cross-training apparel, with the built-in advantage that when you wear them you don't have to spend any time in transition changing out of a swimsuit and into your biking or running apparel.

Outerwear
Remember the 20-degree rule—add 20 degrees (Fahrenheit) to the ambient temperature, and that's how hot it will be during your run. You should dress for the 20-degree rule, keeping in mind that hot weather running requires more consideration than cold, because overheating is more (immediately) dangerous than cold weather exposure. When it's hot, expose as much of your body as you can and wear light, loose-fitting tops. Don't tuck in your shirt, and do wear a visor or cap to shade your face. Also, take care to drink lots of fluids during your workout and run through sprinklers if possible.

Cold weather running is easier, because you can add layers which trap the heat in. A stocking cap and gloves are standard fare. Wear polypro-type (a nickname for polypropolene) blended fabrics for warmth; they also have wicking properties which allow water to escape and warmth to stay in. To combat wet weather, wear waterproof fabrics such as Gore-Tex (which is also breatheable). A run in the cold or in the rain can be as enjoyable as any other—if you dress for success.

Socks

Whether or not to wear socks is a matter of personal preference. Some of my training partners never wear socks, others wear blister-free socks that are double-layered on the bottom. Most runners wear socks for hygenic reasons, since it's easier to wash socks than to wash shoes. Some of you may get blisters if you don't wear socks, some will if you do, and some get them either way.

Make-up

Don't bother with cosmetics before your run—you'll look worse afterwards if you do. Skin care products, though, are an exception. Vaseline can protect your hands and feet from chafing and blistering, and sunscreen is a must if you want to prevent burning—apply it to all exposed areas. Take care of your skin; it is with you for a lifetime.

There is a tradition of female athletes in my family, starting with my grandmother who, like myself, graduated from UC Berkeley. She played on the college basketball team and also ran; I know because her picture appears several times in the 1917 yearbook. In the picture of the basketball team, eight

The year is 1917. The women are competing in the University of California, Berkeley intramural track event. Note the long wool dresses, leather black shoes and hats—the racing activewear of the day.

women are sitting together, with one holding a leather basketball. They are wearing black wool skirts and white blouses—their uniforms.

In the track photo, my grandmother—Gwendolyn Gaynor Roberts—is wearing a long wool skirt, stockings, black flat leather dress shoes, and, of course, a brimmed hat. Her head is thrown back in joy and both arms are pointing towards the sky as if she were victorious, and she would have been, except for the two women in front of her who are breaking the finish line tape.

That was my grandmother—running and finishing in nearly last place and enjoying it. Our foremothers had no training programs, no coaches, no teams, no support, no acceptance, no encouragement, and no proper apparel, but many of them still participated.

I thank you, grandmother, and each and every woman before and after you who paved the way, opened doors, and encouraged us with your examples. I don't think we say thanks enough, so here are a few other thank-you's before we move on.

Thank-you, Melpomene. You broke the taboos when you became the first recorded woman to run a marathon, during the 1896 Olympics. Thank-you—though you scandalized the Greek officials, and you didn't race with the men, you finished the marathon in four hours and 30 minutes, a very impressive time.

Thank-you, Rosie the Riveter—you responded to the needs of our country during World War II, when exercise was elevated to the level of patriotism. Unfortunately, when the men came home and took your jobs, you were misled by the rash of articles on the "dangers" of exercise.

Cheers to the historic passage in 1972 of the landmark law, Title IX, which prohibited discrimination on the basis of sex, in all federally-funded programs. No longer could institutions deny women the right to facilities, budgets, coaches, uniforms, programs, and opportunities.

And hurrah for the acceptance of women as athletes who train for whatever purpose: competition, fun, or conditioning. I look forward to the day when we complete the evolutionary process and the female athlete emerges as a typical 20th-century image in history books—an image which includes large women, minority women, old women, and disabled women, of whatever sexual preference or political viewpoint.

That dream is what drives me to write.

That image is what leads us to train.

Run Training

Keeping in mind the concepts of aerobic and anaerobic training, and of duration, intensity, and distance which we discussed in the last chapter on bicycling, here are a list of different training methods that are commonly used by runners. In the next chapter, we shall combine these methods into your own personalized training program.

Continuous Training

LSD: Long Slow Distances. These are sub-maximal workouts performed at a very low intensity over a very long distance, which are also known as "over-distance" training. Usually, the pace of an LSD workout is slower than your racing speed by at least a minute per mile. The purpose here is to develop long-distance endurance.

Time Trials: A specific distance, at a constant strong intensity, that is timed and used to measure improvement. Time trials are also called pace training, because they teach the triathlete proper pacing.

Aerobics Runs: The training period lasts for 30 minutes to an hour and is usually at a light intensity level. Examples are a five-mile, easy, steady-state run or a fun and relaxed 25-mile time trial on a bike.

Interval Training

Fartlek: Literally translated, fartlek means "speed game." It's a method of training in which there are relatively long-duration, high-intensity periods mixed with low-intensity training (which serve as rest periods), but you still do a continuous workout overall.

Sprints: Maximal effort that lasts 10 to 30 seconds, such as a 100-meter run or 200-meter bike sprint.

Resistance Repeats: These are interval repetitions using a form of resistance for increased workload, such as running up hills (with the rest period being the downhill), running in sand, or running using weights.

Anaerobic Intervals: An intense effort over an extended period of time, commonly from 30 seconds to two minutes. You are stressing your anaerobic system by a near-maximal output. A one-mile bike time trial or a 400-meter run (one lap around a track) are anaerobic interval distances.

Anaerobic Thresholds: This is an interval that lasts from four to 30 minutes and is of above average intensity.

Long Intervals: This involves work periods of two to 15 minutes with intermittent rest periods during the interval. The length of time for the rest is such that you can maintain each of the repeats at a constant rate during the training period. Rest in long-interval training is usually from two to five minutes.

Aerobic and Anaerobic Training Methods

Continuity	Distance "D"	Intensity "I"	Duration "D"	Purpose "DID"
Long Slow Distance	5-20 mi.	Low 60% THR	1-3 hours	Endurance Over-distance
Aerobic Runs	2-5 mi.	Light 70% THR	30 min.-1 hr.	Strength Endurance
Time Trials	3-10 mi.	Moderate 80% THR	20-90 min.	Strength Speed

Interval	"D"	"I"	"D"	"DID"
Sprints	1-3 mi.	Intense 90-100%	10-30 seconds	Speed
Anaerobic Intervals	1-5 mi.	Intense 90-100%	30 sec.-2 min.	Speed Strength
Anaerobic Thresholds	1-6 mi.	Moderate 80-90%	4 min.-30 min.	Anaerobic Power
Resistance Repeats	3-6 mi.	Moderate 80-90%	18-60 min.	Strength
Fartlek	2-8 mi.	Moderate 80% THR	15-80 min.	Strength

PULSE RATE
for Aerobic and Anaerobic Training Methods

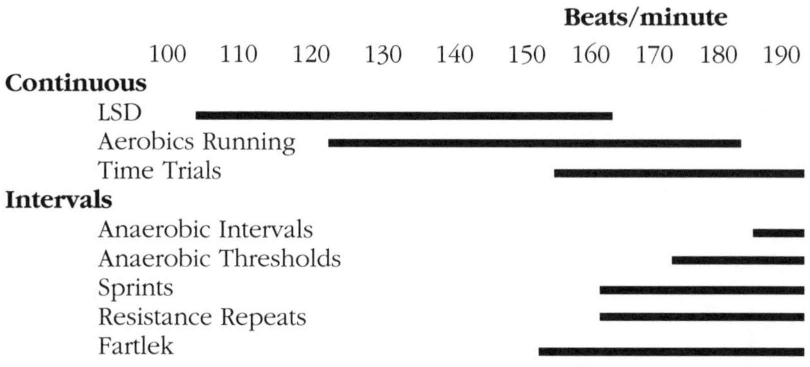

Beats/minute

	100	110	120	130	140	150	160	170	180	190

Continuous

LSD

Aerobics Running

Time Trials

Intervals

Anaerobic Intervals

Anaerobic Thresholds

Sprints

Resistance Repeats

Fartlek

Running through the finish chute of 1990 Ironman Japan, Ironwoman Sally Edwards sets a new master's distance world record of 10 hours and 42 minutes.

5

Train, Don't Exercise—Beginners

Allez. Allez. Allez. Allez.

The French shouted these words at the top of their voices, as I raced over the Alps and through their cobblestone streets during the Nice Triathlon.

Faido. Faido. Faido. Faido.

The Japanese chanted this rhythmically, as I raced through rice paddies and over their narrow macadam streets at the Ironman-Japan.

These words are buried in the center of my brain. I use them frequently when I race and train, for they now have a special motivational meaning for me.

Allez means "let's go." And "go," for the French, is a single word which combines two powerful English words, that all athletes, regardless of sex or race, instinctively use—"go" and "power."

Faido, on the other hand, means "to fight."

Let me explain. As I raced toward the finish line of the Ironman-Japan, the polite Japanese spectators applauded and yelled *faido.* I thought the word meant "second," since that was my position in the field. At the finish line, I asked an English-speaking Japanese triathlete what the word *faido* meant.

She startled me with her answer, since "fighting" was not in my athletic vocabulary; it made me think of doing damage to others. She saw my confusion and said, " 'To fight' to a Japanese means to fight against that inner part of yourself that prevents you from doing your best."

Now I use *allez* whenever I need a boost and *faido* whenever I'm working against myself.

You, too, can use these buzzwords to keep going beyond that first step, those first few weeks of participation in triple fitness. In the beginning, we are easily motivated by health benefits: toned muscles, girth reductions, increased stamina, and cardiovascular improvements. But after the beginning, once you have settled into a routine, you may forget why you began tri-training and wonder why you are putting yourself through so much trouble. In that case, think about the meaning of *faido,* and say *allez* aloud. Let's go!

The Training Program

To use a down-to-earth metaphor, training for triathlons is like preparing, ingesting, and recovering from a major meal. It involves a recipe, ingredients, preparation time, equipment, time planning, labor, measurements, the actual event (eating the meal), clean-up, and rest afterwards. Throughout the training program, as in cooking a meal, there are multiple activities occurring—different pans on the stove at the same time. Welcome to the gourmet training experience!

A 3-course Meal	A Training Program
The Recipe	The Training System
The Ingredients	Training Methods: Continuous and Interval
Amount of Food	Training Volume: the Amount of Training
Cooking Time	Training Cycles: Annual, Seasonal, Monthly, Weekly
Oven Temperature	Training Intensities: Aerobic and Anaerobic
The Chef	The Triathlete
Kitchen Equipment	Training Equipment
Prep Work	Skill and Base Stages
Three Courses	Swim, Bike, Run
Eating	Training
The Best Bite	Peaking Stages
Dessert	Competition
Clean-up	Recovery Stages

Like a good meal, tri-training is especially pleasurable because there is variety among its courses. Each training course or discipline, whether swim, bike, or run, presents its own unique experiences and challenges, yet the training systems that work on one course will apply to the other two. The courses and the obstacles they present vary, but the training system remains the same. Like a well-planned meal, each course complements the next, and all work together toward a spectacular finish!

Questions

I am commonly asked by first-timers (and multi-timers) to answer two questions:

Why train and why compete in trisports?

How much training do I really need to do well?

Since you may be wondering as well, let's break the suspense right now.

Why Should You Begin Tri-training?

Probably the clearest way I can explain *why* is to describe an experience I had during the same Ironman-Japan race that taught me about *faido.* As I reached the turnaround point on the 112-mile bike leg, I saw a banner stretched across the road, the only English banner amongst the hundreds the Japanese had placed along the route.

The banner bore three short words that struck me with the force of a thousand. Their brevity had such an impact that I will carry them with me for the rest of my life.

The banner read: "Do Your Best."

As a woman in triathlon, that's what I want. And that's what I want for you.

The first step is to find the proper ingredients for the training program that is your own recipe.

The second step is to measure them.

How Much Training Do I Need?

Your total yearly training volume will depend on what you want to accomplish and what your goals are. It also depends on a realistic appraisal of the time that you have available and how well you are able to manage the time that you have. Answer this question, "On the average, how much time do I have each day to train?" Then multiply that number times the number of days per week and the number of weeks per year that you are going to train, and you have your annual volume.

Total Yearly   = _____ x _____ x _____
Training Volume   Avg. hours/day   # days/week   # weeks/year

The numbers could look something like this:

1 hour per day x 6 days per week x 40 weeks = 240 hours/year

It might be worth comparing your yearly volume with that of others.

Training Volumes

**Level of
Competitor**   **Hours per year**

	Triathlete	Runner	Swimmer	Cyclist
Professional	800-1400	500-700	400-600	700-1200
Competitor	400-800	300-500	300-400	350-700
Intermediate	300-400	200-300	200-300	200-350
Beginner	<300	<200	<200	<200

The Power of the Distance Training Methods

The amounts of cross-training you'll need to perform (the measurements of your ingredients) depend upon your goals, skills, and physiological state. So, on a very subtle, personal level, I can't presume to tell you how much to train. However, there is an easy formula which you can use to find the approximate training volume you will need—you take the lengths of the event in which you wish to compete and make your training distances a multiple of the racing distances.

Let's take the Danskin Triathlon Series distances of 1k swim, 20k bike and 5k run, which are the standard lengths for a "sprint" triathlon. Just because the distances are short doesn't mean that the race is easy—most women trade the shorter distances for faster speeds, so the effort remains demanding.

Next, take a multiplying factor and apply it to those distances. Let's use 3 as the multiplier for our purposes here. Then, to determine your weekly training volume, multiply the following sprint distances by three, and that will equal your weekly training distance.

Formula: Multiple x Distances   = Total Distance to Train per Week

$$
\begin{aligned}
3 \times 1\text{k swim} &= 3\text{k swim per week} \\
3 \times 20\text{k bike} &= 60\text{k bike per week} \\
3 \times 5\text{k run} &= 15\text{k run per week}
\end{aligned}
$$

This is called the "The Power of Distance" training system. Using the Power of the Distance, your total weekly volume would be 3k (just under two miles) of swimming, 60k (37 miles) on your bike, and 15k (nine miles) of running.

How much time would it take you to train at the Power of Three? Let's figure that out and see if you can fit it into the amount of time you have available.

The easiest way is to break these distances into parts, time the parts, and then multiply the result by the total distance. For example, if you can comfortably swim 100 meters in two minutes, then swimming 3,000 meters per week (30 times as far) would take you 60 minutes a week (30 times as long).

1. Swim: _____ minutes per 100 meters x 30 = _____minutes

2. Bike: _____ kilometers per hour divided into 60 k = _____ hours

3. Run: _____ minutes per kilometer x 15 k = _____minutes

Let's now look at a novice triathlete. Does she have enough time in a week to train at the level of the power of three? Let's find out:

1. Swim: 2 minutes x 30 = *60 minutes*

2. Bike: 26 kph divided into 60 k = *2 hours and 18 minutes*

3. Run: 5 minutes/k x 15 k = *1 hour and 15 minutes*

Total weekly training time = *4 hours and 33 minutes*
Average daily workout time = *38 minutes per day*

Figure it out for yourself—it's easy to do. In our example, you need to train an average of 38 minutes per day to be in tri-shape and to successfully complete a sprint-distance triathlon. That's not a particularly large amount of time, so you will simply need to organize your priorities to fit in that 38-minute period each day. If you want to train only six days a week, that's fine, too. Your average daily workout time will still be only 46 minutes per day, if you want to take a day off during your week.

Here are the tables for determining your various training volumes, based on the Power of the Distance. Start your first several weeks at Level One and progress when the hunger gets stronger and the workouts seem easier; your rate of progression is as much based upon subjective information as objective.

Training Schedules
Power of the Distance

				Approximate Daily Time
Level 1: Novice (Train at this level for 2-4 weeks)				
Power of 1:	1 k swim	20 k bike	5 k run	14 min
Level 2: Initiate (Train here for 4-8 weeks)				
Power of 2:	2 k swim	40 k bike	10 k run	27 min
Level 3: Experienced Beginner (Train at this level until you are ready to move to the next stage—Intermediate)				
Power of 3:	3 k swim	60 k bike	15 k run	38 min
Level 4: Intermediate (Train here for 4-12 weeks)				
Power of 4:	4 k swim	80 k bike	20 k run	53 min
Level 5: Advanced (At this stage and above, how far and how fast you advance is up to you—go for it!)				
Power of 5:	5 k swim	100 k bike	25 k run	66 min
Level 6: Competitor				
Power of 6:	6 k swim	120 k bike	30 k run	80 min
Level 7: Elite or Pro				
Power of 7:	7 k swim	140 k bike	35 k run	1.5 hrs
Power of 8:	8 k swim	160 k bike	40 k run	1.75 hrs
Power of 9:	9 k swim	180 k bike	45 k run	2 hrs
Level 8: Ironwoman				
Power of 10	10 k swim	200 k bike	50 k run	over 2 hrs

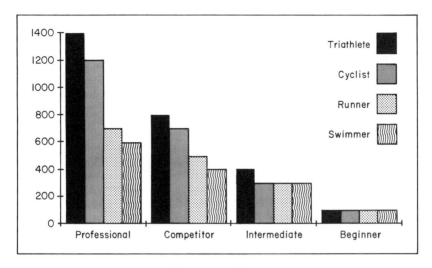

Training Volumes

As you become more dedicated to tri-training and your fitness level grows, you will consider increasing your weekly training levels to the Power of 4 or the Power of 5 training systems.   At this point, you are ready to consider racing longer than sprint-distance races and you will have become an "intermediate" triathlete.

A goal can be setting a finish time on a clock—and matching it.

6

Train, Don't Exercise— Intermediates

Welcome to the union of fit women who have passed the first hurdle of lifetime athleticism—the novice or beginner stage. You have promoted yourself to the class of tri-women who have made a commitment to the sport and who are taking their level of experience to new heights.

You are in the middle of an evolutionary process: from beginner to intermediate to competitor. As you approach each higher level, new parameters to training will be added. You will also need to understand more of the training principles and have a higher level of appreciation for the intricacies of performance training.

As a beginner, you were testing the triathletic waters. You may have been exercising, more than training, working out for the purpose of gaining fitness, not necessarily working to gain fitness in order to meet a goal beyond. You have now hit the point where you've realized that training has purpose. This is the level where you make the transition from saying "Yes, I am into training" to "I am training for (something)." The word "for" indicates that you have intent. Let me show you. Get something to write with, and don't read any further until you have a pen or pencil in hand.

Now, fill in the following blanks by stating the answer to this question: "What do I want to accomplish from training?"

1. I am training for _____

2. I am also training for _____

3. I would like to train for _____

    Stop. If you decided to just pass by those three statements, you made a mistake. Go back and fill them in now. It is important that you do that before you read the next paragraph. Please.

    The "training for" separates the trainers from the exercisers, because it means that you have a goal, that you want to accomplish something. If you are into fitness for staying in shape, then you are a member of the exercise community. However, if you are into fitness for accomplishing something—learning more about yourself, meeting new friends, expanding your horizons, entering a race, or beating a nemesis—then you train, you don't exercise.

    As you take the steps from beginner to intermediate to competitor, you put aside exercise and learn about new training principles such as:

- Big and Little Goals
- The Four Cycles: Annual, Seasonal, Monthly, and Weekly

    Together, these principles will lead you into your own individualized training schedule.

Big and Little Goals

    Remember, goals are what separate a trainer from an exerciser. Your big goals are what you wrote as your "training for" answers, and they will help you determine the framework of your annual and seasonal cycles. But, there are also little goals, sometimes called objectives, that are the steps to accomplishing the big goals, and these are what monthly and weekly cycles focus on.

    Still, I firmly believe you always need to keep the big goal in mind. It's like having an elephant in your garden, trampling your violets. You could work on completing a little goal—protecting your violets—by fencing the flowers off with chicken wire. However, since elephants aren't chickens, that probably won't work very well. What would work would be to focus on your big goal—getting rid of the elephant—by calling your local zoo. To put it briefly, give your attention to the elephants in your life, and your violets will grow beautifully.

The Four Cycles

Definitions:

1) Annual Cycles: One year periods of training and training goals.

2) Seasonal Cycles: Periods of two to eight months duration which together form an annual cycle. Each seasonal cycle consists of six training stages.

3) Monthly Cycles: These are four week periods which focus on one of the six training stages of the seasonal cycle.

4) Weekly Cycles: Seven day training periods, four of which comprise a monthly cycle.

Annual Cycles

The annual cycle is probably one of the most diffcult to formulate because it means that you must look forward into the future. To design an annual cycle you need to answer this question: Athletically, what would I like to accomplish this year and the next year(s)?

An annual cycle gives you the opportunity to plan your athletics over the long term. An example of an annual cycle would be to set your first year of training as a learning experience, one in which you would like to finish one triathlon. In your second annual cycle, you might like to train and enter five triathlons of both sprint and international distance and complete a century bike ride. In cycle year three, you might want to finish a long course triathlon and attempt your first marathon.

Write down a few annual goals in the following chart:

ANNUAL CYCLE

Year	19___	19___	19___
G 1			
O			
A 2			
L			
S 3			

Seasonal Cycles

These are the big pictures in performance training, your maps of your big training goals and time lines. Some triathletes draw a training map based on seasons of the year—spring, summer, fall, and winter—making four seasonal cycles. Others prefer to divide their year into as many as seven seasonal cycles, based on their racing schedules.

I am a two season cycler: eight months of the year I race in triathlons and four months of the year I run in road races. Seasonal cycles are usually from two to six months in length and are individually tailored to your type of athleticism.

Divide the months of the year up, based on what you want to accomplish. For example, you should note when you plan on recuperating, traveling, the specific races you have scheduled, and the different sports activities you will be training for. All this should begin to give you an idea of how to set up your yearly seasonal plan.

Seasonal Cycle Plan

Month	Plan
January:	
February:	
March:	
April:	
May:	
June:	
July:	
August:	
September:	
October:	
November:	
December:	

Monthly Cycles

Monthly cycles are four week periods which are usually dedicated to improving one major factor of your performance—for example, speed. A series of monthly cycles will form a progression, from base training to post-race recovery, which, when united, form a season.

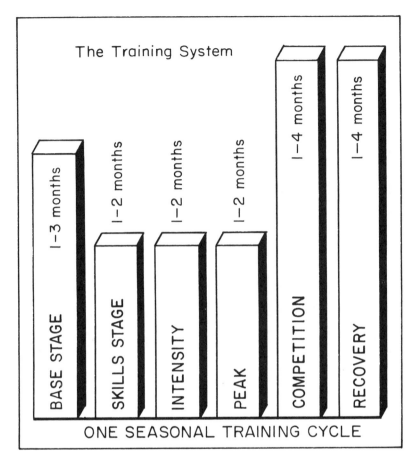

The Training System

BASE STAGE — 1–3 months

SKILLS STAGE — 1–2 months

INTENSITY — 1–2 months

PEAK — 1–2 months

COMPETITION — 1–4 months

RECOVERY — 1–4 months

ONE SEASONAL TRAINING CYCLE

The Six Monthly Stages

Training is a progression—a series of little steps that lead you to the completion of your goals. Whatever your annual and seasonal training goals, the little steps that it takes to get there are the six different monthly stages: base, skills, intensity, peak, competition, and recovery. Each stage lasts one (or more, if you need or wish) months.

The Base Stage: 1–3 months (4–12 weeks)

This is a cycle of low intensity and low training volume, when you lay down the foundation to your training program. Exercise physiologists call this the "aerobic buildup phase," because you are training for the aerobic, not the anaerobic, component of fitness. The cycle consists of workouts that are easy

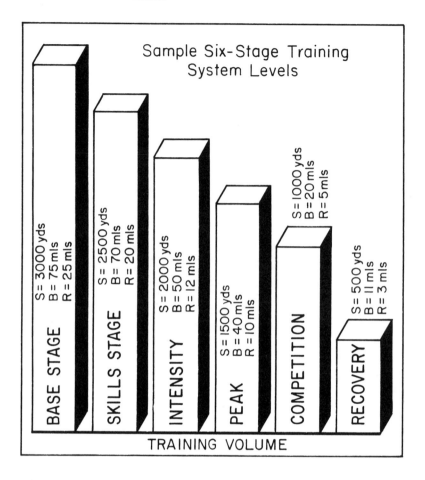

Sample Six-Stage Training System Levels

BASE STAGE — S = 3000 yds / B = 75 mls / R = 25 mls

SKILLS STAGE — S = 2500 yds / B = 70 mls / R = 20 mls

INTENSITY — S = 2000 yds / B = 50 mls / R = 12 mls

PEAK — S = 1500 yds / B = 40 mls / R = 10 mls

COMPETITION — S = 1000 yds / B = 20 mls / R = 5 mls

RECOVERY — S = 500 yds / B = 11 mls / R = 3 mls

TRAINING VOLUME

and continuous, and which lead to strength and stamina, not necessarily speed, although you will need to introduce some speedwork into the later weeks. This is also a stage of developing strength, so include weight workouts with machines or free weights as well as sport-specific strength workouts, such as running and cycling hills.

The Skills Stage: 1–2 months (4–8 weeks)

This is a cycle of sport-specific training, for the purpose of improving your technique. It is a time to fine-tune your swim, bike, and run biomechanics—to concentrate on developing the movement skills more than the endurance skills. Read several sport-specific books such as *The Woman Runner* (Gloria Averbuch, 1984), *The Woman Cyclists* (Elaine Mariolle, 1988),

The Bodywise Woman (Melpomene Institute, 1990), and *The Fit Swimmer* (Marianne Brens, 1988), because studying the mechanics of sports really does lead to enhanced biomechanical efficiency. Approximately 80 percent of your training volume during this cycle will be aerobic and over-distance training.

The Intensity Stage: 1–2 months (4–8 weeks)

This is a demanding and vigorous cycle. You take the base and skills you've developed over the prior two stages and add intensity training. This period will usually include the highest training volume of any monthly cycle. Approximately 50 to 60 percent of your training volume will still be LSD, aerobic training, and aerobic time trials. The balance needs to be in interval training, such as time trials, fartleks, resistance repeats, and anaerobic intervals. This is a time for you to enter an individual sport race such as a 5 k road race or a bike time trial.

The Peak Stage: 1–2 months (4–8 weeks)

This is a short stage built around sharpening specific workouts, which are characterized by lower-distance training at higher-intensity volumes. Physiologically, you are stressing your energy systems at high speeds in order to gain speed, as well as to refine your technique. Some coaches refer to this as "sharpening." It is called "peaking" because of the decrease in training volume, yet it is a "sharpening" because of the refinement component.

The Competition Stage: 1–4 months (4–16 weeks)

This is the stage when you are capable of racing at your best. I think of it as the dessert of training, because it is such a delicious stage to a competitive athlete. Over half of the training during this stage will be over-distance training, and this is a time to actively train while in the midst of a racing schedule and what it entails (travel, diet changes, psychological stress). Maintaining your aerobic base should be central to your planning. Interval training should represent 10-15% of the training volume.

The Recovery Stage: 1–4 months (4–16 weeks)

This is the rest phase of training, when you can gain weight and slow down. Training in this stage is of very low intensity and moderate to low volume. It is a stage when sport-specific training is unimportant—take up new activities such as cross-country skiing, rollerblades, or aerobic dancing. It is an active restoration period—you might enjoy sports like volleyball or softball and working on your team playing skills. Enjoy the recovery stage and stay active.

Weekly Cycles

Your Training Schedule

The reason that you design your own training schedules is that training is an individualized program—what works for you, only works for you, and not for anyone else.

As an example, a swim coach writes a workout for her team to perform. On the team of 30 swimmers, three are stars and the remainder perform adequately, but not as well. Why? There are a number of reasons, but probably the one that fits is that the coach has designed a training program that is working for only those three swimmers, the other 27 need a different program—one that works for them.

For you to create your training program, you will need a way to write it down—a sample format, a worksheet, a template, an outline. You already have most of the information that you need to fill in the blanks—what you are missing is the swim-bike-run workout for each individual training day.

At the end of this chapter, you will find a worksheet called a tri-training template which includes all of the information that you need to successfully plan each week of your monthly cycles as well as each individual training day. I've included both a filled-out sample template and a blank one for your use.

Fill in the Blanks

You have all the information that you need to complete this tri-training template. You know your weekly training volume from the Power of the Distance formula (see Chapter 5, Beginners). You can decide how many workouts per week that you can invest, by looking at your time availability. For example, if you can only train five days a week and there is only one time slot for that workout, then the answer to the Total Number of Workouts per Week is pretty simple—"five."

You must now write each day's training schedules. To determine specific workouts, refer back to the sections on training in each of "The Basic Moves" chapters.

Tri-Training Template

Training for Goal **DO WELL AT BLTS – Baltimore**
Seasonal Cycle Period **January 1 – July 30**
Number of Seasonal Cycle Months/Weeks **8 months = 32 weeks**
Week Number **10**
Cycle Goal **INTENSITY**
Power of the Distance **#3**
Total Weekly Training Volume **3k swim / 60k bike / 15k run**
Total Number of Workouts per Week **6 workouts**

SEASONAL STAGES

Base: **4** weeks
Skills: **4** weeks
Intensity: **8** weeks
Peak: **4** weeks
Compete: **8** weeks
Recovery: **4** weeks
Total: **32** weeks

DAY		SPORT	VOLUME	WORKOUT	Interval	High Intensity
MON	am / pm	Swim	1000k	WARM UP 1x300 EASY / MAINSET 5x100 @ 2:00 MIN / COOL DOWN 1x200 EASY	500 M	60% EASY
TUES	am / pm	BIKE	20k	Ride 12 miles with a 5 miles easy and 10 min of intervals	10 min	80%
WED	am / pm	RUN	5k	Run easy with my run partner		70%
THURS	am / pm			REST		
FRI	am / pm	SWIM	2000k	WARM UP 1x500 EASY / MAIN SET 3x150 2x100 10x50 / COOL DOWN 1x350		80%
SAT	am / pm	BIKE	40k	Ride with the Saturday moring bike group – meet @ 10 a.m. and try to stay with them – I won't be dropped		75%
SUN	am / pm	RUN	10k	Fun run Do my hardest & best		100%

Tri-Training Template

Training for Goal _____

Seasonal Cycle Period _____

Number of Seasonal Cycle Months/Weeks _____ months = _____ weeks

Week Number _____

Cycle Goal _____

Power of the Distance _____

Total Weekly Training Volume _____

Total Number of Workouts per Week _____

SEASONAL STAGES

Base: _____ weeks

Skills: _____ weeks

Intensity: _____ weeks

Peak: _____ weeks

Compete: _____ weeks

Recovery: _____ weeks

Total: _____ weeks

DAY		SPORT	VOLUME	WORKOUT	Interval	High Intensity
MON	am					
	pm					
TUES	am					
	pm					

	am	pm
W		
THURS	am	pm
FRI	am	pm
SAT	am	pm
SUN	am	pm

I know that writing your own weekly and monthly cycle training programs is not easy, but I guarantee that a systematic training program like this achieves two major goals: you get the most out of your training, and you do it in the least amount of time. If you dedicate the time to planning out your schedule, the return is enormous.

To help you, I have created a sample graph which shows possible training volume levels for each of the six monthly stages. Study them, then become an accomplished intermediate by taking charge of your training and writing your own workouts. Photocopy the blank tri-training template and complete one for each week. Finally, post the tri-training templates in a conspicuous place, such as the mirror in your bathroom, so that you are always reminded of your plans.

Training Log

The tri-training template resembles a training log, except that the template looks at what you are going to do, not what you've actually done or how it went. That is the purpose of my Triathlon Log; it is a record of the training that you have completed, both quantitatively and qualitatively. In other words, you can use the Tri Log as your own private training diary—you can admit to your problems and your revelations, workouts missed, difficulties encountered, and personal records set.

You can purchase copies of the Triathlon Log by writing my office: *FLEET FEET, INCORPORATED*, 2408 "J" Street, Sacramento, CA 95816 or by calling (916) 442-3338. They are $7.95 each, including shipping and handling, and take about two weeks to be received. The Triathlon Log is also available in sports retail stores around the country.

DATE	SPORT	DISTANCE	TIME	TYPE WKOUT	PULSE	HRS. SLEEP WEIGHT MOOD			COMMENTS
						HRS	LBS		
M									
T						HRS	LBS		
W						HRS	LBS		
T						HRS	LBS		
F						HRS	LBS		
S						HRS	LBS		
S						HRS	LBS		

WEEK #		SWIM	BICYCLE	RUN	COMMENTS:
	Total Distance For Week				
	Total Training Hrs.				
	Distance Year To Date				

The Triathlon Log, your official record and diary. To order, write or call FLEET FEET Press at 2408 "J" Street, Sacramento, CA 95316 (916-442-3338).

┌─────────┐
│ **7** │
└─────────┘

Train, Don't Exercise—
Competitor

Women haven't begun to reach the limits of their performance—athletically, psychologically, or otherwise. The range of growth possible is one of the most exciting components to women's athletics—women are not just breaking through barriers, but instead are crashing them down loudly.

While athletic performance improvements for men are at a near standstill, the same is not the case for women. As the monetary rewards for women's competition have increased, those women who had previously trained as a hobby can now afford to dedicate themselves to it.

Triathlon is an excellent example. From 1981 to 1985, I placed in the top five in the women's open division at the Ironman World Triathlon Championships (with one second, two thirds, and two fifth place finishes). In 1986, the race first offered a prize purse of a then-substantial sum of money— $100,000. For that kind of reward, women began to train to new dimensions, and there was a quantum leap in the quality of triathletic women who were attracted to compete. So that year, in 1986, I finished 35th.

I was definitely disappointed with my finish, but I was so proud of the professionalism I saw that my disappointments were completely canceled out.

That takes me to my reasons for writing all this.

I could have written a lightweight triathlon training book

1990 Sacramento Triathlon winner Erin Baker. Another first for her—she and husband Scott Molina won both the women's and men's pro divisions respectively in the same race.

for women, kept it simple and filled it with fluff, assuming that you, my reader, just wanted something easy to digest, with schedules that told you what to do every day.

I respect you too much to do that.

I believe that triathletic women are the advance guard of a new group of 21st-century females—women who love sports for their intrinsic value and who take sports seriously.

This chapter is for the serious triathletic woman (or man), not for the light of heart. This systematic training plan is for the triathlete who wants to do the best that she possibly can, regardless of the factors she cannot control—her genetic disposition (for speed, endurance, agility, and flexibility). You can't change genetics, but you can maximize your potential, and one of the best ways to do so is to utilize advanced training principles.

Please stop if this description of the "competitor" doesn't match you—it's OK. This chapter isn't written for everyone. Just skip ahead to the next chapters where I deal with important topics such as triathlon medicine, motivation, and meaning. You can come back to this chapter later on, if you wish.

But if you want to engage in the most comprehensive level of tri-training, I suggest you read and reread this chapter, because it takes training to a higher, faster plane.

Here are the concepts and practices you need to add to the intermediate level of training in order to be a competitor:

- workload;
- periodization;
- doubles and triples;
- daily intensity.

I believe that competitive triathletic women take their sports seriously. If you do and if you want more details on Serious Training for Serious Athletes, I urge you to read the book of that title by Rob Sleamaker (1989, Leisure Press). It's one of the best that I have read in the last decade. But start by reading this chapter right here.

Workload

Workload is a concept that combines the amount (or the volume or quantity) and intensity (the quality) of stress applied in a specific training bout. For example, if you are swimming, and the individual workout calls for 5 x 200 easy and 10 x 100 anaerobic (hard) intervals, the workload is 2,000 yards with 50 percent easy and 50 percent hard. If the next day you run 5 repeat one miles at a fast 7 minute per mile time, with a two minute rest, your workload is five interval/hard miles, at a 3.5 to 1 work-to-rest ratio.

Periodization

When I was training for the 1984 Olympic Marathon Trials, after barely qualifying with a 2:50 finish at the Phoenix Marathon, I used a training cycle called hard/easy days. One day I would run hard, which always meant either short or long intervals, and the next day I would run easy or continuous easy, which was usually long-distance training.

A more advanced application of hard/easy training is a principle called periodization, a training system that varies the intensity and the amount (volume) of training within an individual monthly cycle. Periodization is well-suited to a body's own cycles of exertion and recovery, and allows the body to spend time both resting and training hard, when that is what's necessary. The periods are groups of workouts that gradually improve fitness level (base) and increase sharpness for competition (peaks).

As an example, let's say that a training stage is planned over a two month period. During those eight weeks, you structure a period of three weeks that build (hard), with a fourth week that is easy, followed by a three-week period that builds to a new fitness level, which in turn is followed by a one-week recuperation period. Periodization can be graphed as follows:

Periodization of a Training Stage

— High Training Intensity (Quality)
+++ High Training Volume (Quantity)

```
                    Weekly Breakdown of Month's Total
Week   1    ++++++++———————23%
       2    ++++———————————— 27%
       3    +++++++++++++————————————32%
       4    +++++++++++++—18%   (recuperation period)
                 100% for the month

Week   5    +++++++++———————20%
       6    +++++++++++++————————————————30%
       7    +++++++++++++————————————————————35%
       8    ++——————————15% (recuperation period)
                 100% for the month
```
Percent of High Intensity and High Volume Work Loads in
One Month Cycles

Periodization allows a progressive increase in the intensity and volume of the workload, resulting in quicker exercise adaptation. During the first three weeks of the monthly cycle, the body adapts by gaining fitness; during the fourth week it adapts to the rest period by recuperating, so that it can accept greater workloads during the next four-week period of the monthly cycle.

In periodization, training loads and intensities are increased progressively, so that the body adapts and improves, instead of breaking down or weakening. However, not everyone adapts best to the same periodization pattern. Experiment here. Try alternating weeks in a 30%-20%-30%-20% periodization, especially if you race every two weeks with the race falling on the easy (20 percent) weeks. Feel absolutely free to shape the periodization cycle so that it fits your training and racing schedule.

Double and Triple Workouts

One of the ways to increase training volume is to increase the number of individual workouts in one day. A beginner should be training four to six times weekly, with no more than one workout each day and at least one full day of total rest within each week. An intermediate triathlete adds to their training volume by increasing both training distance and the number of training sessions. An intermediate should still take one day of rest per week, but might choose to progress from six workouts per week to 10, by adding multiple workouts during one or more days. Competitors usually average between 1 1/2 and 2 1/2 workouts per day, adding up to a week that consists of 9 to 14 training sessions.

In determining which sports to combine on double workout days, consider your daily schedule so that training fits into your home and professional lifestyle. Since running and cycling both require lower body stress, I recommend that you rarely combine them and instead add swimming, an upper body skill, as the second workout of the day. Here is a training pattern that includes 9 workouts per week:

Day	Swim	Bike	Run	Single Double Days	Number of Workouts
1	x		x	D	2
2			x	S	1
3	———————Rest———————				0
4	x		x	D	2
5			x	S	1
6			x	S	1
7	x	x		D	2
					Total: 9 Workouts

Adding triple workout days requires planning (especially since few of us are full-time triathletes). Triple days are usually part of your day off work or school, because they are time-demanding. Back-to-back triples (performing all three workouts with no rest between them) resemble a triathlon time trial and are only recommended if you want to train for the transition or to simulate racing conditions. Otherwise, it is best to rest between each workout on double or triple workout days—it allows your metabolic reserves to re-build and to enhance each individual workload session.

When you have progressed to triple workout days, you need to intensely tune into your body and its signals. There are side effects to overtraining, just as there are to undertraining, and you need to pay heed to potential problems from overuse or misuse of your body.

Daily Intensity Training

How do triathletes like Colleen Cannon, Karen Smyers, and Sara Springman train at high aerobic and anaerobic training volumes and continue each year to get faster—breaking new records and moving the outer boundaries of triathlon further and further?

Clearly, professionals train with high training volumes, some as high as 1,400 hours per year. They didn't start there, though; they trained up to that volume. They have reached their current fitness potentials by gradual physiological development and refinement of their biomechanical skills, studying strategy, developing personally, and maturing physically. There is one additional reason pros can train to such heights—cross-training itself.

The nature of triathlon is such that it offers the opportunity to alternate high-intensity training sessions on a daily basis. For example, one day you train hard (i.e., with high intensity) in swimming (not using your running or biking muscles), the next day hard in cycling (resting your swimming and running muscle groups), and the next day hard in running (rest your swimming and cycling muscle groups). In this way, you can train hard in one skill every day, but you will alternate your training in such a way that the sport-specific muscles of two systems always get at least a day of rest. Your cardiorespiratory system gains fitness, while you are simultaneously resting alternate muscle groups.

In a 14-workout week, with three double days and two triple days, this is how daily hard or high-intensity training is scheduled:

High Intensity Workouts

I= Intense
E = Easy

Day	Swim	Bike	Run	Intense Workload	Single Double Triple	Number Workouts
1	I	E		I	D	2
2	E		I	I	D	2
3		I		I	S	1
4	I	E	E	I	T	3
5			I	I	S	1
6	E	I	E	I	T	3
7	I	E		I	D	2
				7 Hard Workouts		Total: 14 Workouts

Tri-training Template Plan

To complete the competitive triathletes' training template, you must add these new components to your schedule: periodization, multiple daily workouts, and daily high-intensity workloads.

Periodization. During the first four weeks of a monthly cycle, increase the training volume for the first three, and then reduce it for the purpose of recuperation in the fourth. Here are some sample four-week periodization patterns:

Week 1   2   3   4
23%-26%-29%-22% = 100% of four week training cycle
22%-27%-33%-18% = 100%
23%-28%-30%-28% = 100%
25%-25%-30%-20% = 100%
25%-25%-30%-20% = 100%
25%-25%-25%-25% = 100%

Multiple Workouts: Progressively increase from one double workout per week to several, eventually adding your first triple workout to your week's schedule. Start with six workouts per week and progressively add a workout until you reach your goal.

Daily Intensity: Select one of the three sports as your intensity activity for the day. And remember to alternate between all three on different days, so your conditioning will be balanced.

The following are a completed "Competitor" level tri-training template which you can use as a model in designing your own as well as a blank one. Note that the only difference between the intermediate triathlete and the competitor is the addition of these three new competitor-level components.

A Special Note to Competitors

A training philosophy that I have followed for over twenty years of successful racing can be summarized in two stanzas.

> If you want to race fast, train fast.
> If you want to race slow, train slow.
> If you want to race well, learn pace.
> If you want to race well until you die,
>   pace yourself over a lifetime.

> You may want it today.
> You probably will get it tomorrow.
> Systematically plan for it.
> Systematically train for it.
> It can be yours.

Competitive Tri-Training Template

Training for Goal __OLD SACRAMENTO TRIATHLON__

Seasonal Cycle Period __INTENSITY__

Number of Seasonal Cycle Months/Weeks __4½__ months = __18__ weeks

Week Number __#9__

Cycle Goal __GET FITTER and FASTER ; Add several double workouts__

Power of the Distance __#7__

Total Weekly Training Volume Swim : __7,750__   Bike : __105 mls__   Run : __35 mls .__

Total Number of Workouts per Week __11__   # Doubles __4__   # Triples __0__

Periodization Pattern __22 %__   _____ % week

SEASONAL STAGES

Base:	_____ weeks
Skills:	_____ weeks
Intensity:	_____ weeks
Peak:	_____ weeks
Compete:	_____ weeks
Recovery:	_____ weeks
Total:	_____ weeks

TRAINING STAGE PERIODIZATION PATTERN

	Wk 1	Wk 2	Wk 3	Wk 4	
					= 100% month
					= 100% month
					= 100% month
					= 100% month
					= 100% month
					= 100% month
					= 100% month

Workout Table

DAY		SPORT	VOLUME	WORKOUT	INTERVAL	INTENSITY
MON	am	BIKE	25 mls	Warmup easy 5 mls - then 2 min "on" @ 160 beats/min 2 min "off" 30 min	15 × 2 min	160 beats/min.
	pm	SWIM	1,600 yds	Warmup - 500 yds free. Main set 10×100 @ 1:55 , 1 × 100 cool down	10 × 100	@ 1:55
TUES	am	RUN	10 mls.	Warmup - 1 ml. slow, 5×1 ml. @ 6:10 pace , ¼ ml. run - rest between	5 × 1	6:10 pace
	pm					
WED	am	BIKE	30 mls	Training ride - ½ hr. warmup, then 15 mls. hard paceline - ride pace		22 mph @ 170 beats/min
	pm	SWIM	3,200 yds	Warmup - 500 yds.; 1×1000 @ race pace, cool down stretch 500 yds.	1 × 1,000	on 30 min/mile pace
THURS	am	RUN	8 mls	Steady continuous run @ 7:00 min. pace on measured course - learn pace	1 × 8 mls.	Sub anaerobic
	pm					
FRI	am	SWIM	2,500 yds	Warmup - mixed strokes 500 yds; main set 10×200 yds @ 4 min, cool down	10 × 200	on the 4 min.
	pm	RUN	5 mls	Easy fartleks - run 30 seconds, rest, 60 seconds for 3 miles	3 mls.	very fast
SAT	am	BIKE	50 mls	Fun ride in the country with friends - "TIME IN THE SADDLE"		
	pm					
SUN	am	SWIM	1,650 yds	Warmup 1×250; main set - ladder 1×100, 2×150, 3×200, 2×150, 1×100 cool down	LADDERS	
	pm	RUN	12 mls	Long run day - steady / EASY PACE		

Competitive Tri-Training Template

Training for Goal _____

Seasonal Cycle Period _____

Number of Seasonal Cycle Months/Weeks _____ months = _____

Week Number _____

Cycle Goal _____

Power of the Distance _____

Total Weekly Training Volume _____

Total Number of Workouts per Week _____ # Doubles _____ # Triples

Periodization Pattern _____

DAY		SPORT			VOLUME	WORKC
MON	am					
	pm					
TUES	am					
	pm					
WED	am					
	pm					
THURS	am					
	pm					
FRI	am					
	pm					
SAT	am					
	pm					
SUN	am					
	pm					

SEASONAL STAGES

Base: _____ weeks

Skills: _____ weeks

Intensity: _____ weeks

Peak: _____ weeks

Compete: _____ weeks

Recovery: _____ weeks

Total: _____ weeks

% week

TRAINING STAGE PERIODIZATION PATTERN

Wk 1	Wk 2	Wk 3	Wk 4	
				= 100% month
				= 100% month
				= 100% month
				= 100% month

	INTERVAL	INTENSITY

Racing always begins with a starting line. So does training. . .

8

Racing

Getting yourself to the finish line of a race may be one of your "big goals." If so, I'd like to help you get there. If not, I'd like to encourage you to reconsider. Racing can be as big or as small a step as you make it. You can aim toward competing in an Ironman (as an Iron*woman*) or simply sign up for your next local "Tri for Fun" (these are usually short, relatively noncompetitive events). In any case, be reasonable with yourself. Success at racing always involves an honest evaluation of your own strengths and weaknesses, as well as setting realistic goals.

You'll want to break the race into five parts—three separate sporting events connected by two transitions. Think of each event as having an individual starting and finish line (they do!). Then, link three great races together with two fast and efficient transitions.

Prevent failure by preparing well—be meticulous with your equipment, hydrate before the race, and eat and sleep well during the days and nights before.

Warm up your mind before the race, as well as your body. Think through the whole race day so thoroughly that you know the race as well as if you had already completed it. This will in large part eliminate the pre-race jitters.

Acknowledge that there will be pain. Exhaustion and discomfort are part of the entry fee that's paid to attain peak performance, so go ahead and pay the price, but only up to a point. When you near the point where pain is verging on bodily overextension or breakdown, back-off. It's better to finish upright than to practice the "triathloid crawl."

Tap into and refine the source of your energy—the mind/body union. Listen intently to both the sounds of your mind's chatter and the feelings of your heart and lung exertion. Fine-tune both to maximize your efficiency, and relax into the experience as best as you can.

Grow from the race. If you have a disaster, a broken bike, a slow swim, or a fat man who passes you, use those experiences for what they were meant to be: lessons. Link the lessons together, and you will watch your performance grow.

Lastly, remember to live it up. Racing is like a big par-ty—the actual event may be the main attraction, but the sideshow is almost as much fun. Meet new people, share sto-ries, eat, drink, and be the merriest of them all—you deserve it.

The Heart of the Matter: Transitions

The heart of triathlons are the transitions between the events, the swim-to-bike and the bike-to-run. If you've come to the point in your training where you've developed sufficient skill and endurance in each of the three sports to consider entering a race, knowing how to transition efficiently will be the last piece in your winning puzzle.

Add proper transition preparation to your training pro-gram. Take a swim and transition onto a bike ride and, like-wise, ride and transition onto a run. Mental preparation is important, so visualize yourself moving through each step in an orderly fashion, and it will become a familiar experience.

At the Danskin Triathlon Series-New York race, I watched a woman walk up the shoot to the bike transition area after the swim, the last finisher out of 600 plus women. I don't know her name—she was one of hundreds of women immersed in their first triathlon. She met two of her supporters there who had managed to get into the transition area to help her, and she said to the two friends, "I can't believe I did it." It was one of the happiest moments of her life—she hadn't known if she could swim that far, in open water, in a strange lake, with hun-dreds of other triathletic women, but she did it. "I have never

Racing always ends with some kind of a finish line.

been so scared in my whole life," she confided. Now that the swim leg was completed, she wasn't worried about the 20k bike and the 5k run.

There was no urgency in her actions. She sat down and ate a sandwich, chatted with her friends about the joy and thrill of her accomplishments, and she finally left the swim-to-bike transition area about 10 minutes later.

Meanwhile, Fernanda Keller, the Danskin-sponsored pro triathlete, transitioned in 45 seconds. She was totally focused on time, not socializing, because she needed to catch Lisa Laiti, who had been first out of the transition area. Lisa crashed on her bike soon after, though, and didn't finish the race. But the last-place woman swimmer did finish—she may not have tried to catch anyone on the bike leg, and she probably ran and walked the 5k run. But she did it—she finished.

How to Get Organized for Transitions

You'll find it helps to plan your transitions in advance. Write a list of all the equipment that you may need and save it for future reference. Here's my complete list, but since everyone is different, just keep a list that fits you:

Swim	Bike	Run
Racing suit	Helmet	Running shoes
Goggles	Bike	Visor
Towel	Bike accessories	
Gear bag	Sunglasses	*Optional:*
Swim cap	Shoes/cleats	Socks
Optional:	Race number	Sunscreen
Wetsuit	Water bottles	Running shorts
Goggle		Food
defogger	*Optional:*	
Trisuit	Safety Pins	
	Cycling shorts	
	Food	
	Water bucket to rinse feet	
	Socks	
	Cycling gloves	
	Fanny Pack	
	Vaseline	

Putting the Pieces Together: Race Day

Transition Set-Up

The morning of the race, arrive an hour early so that you can test your gear, go through your body marking (a number will be written on you with felt pens), take care of calls from nature, relax, and stretch.

In the bike transition area, numbered racks will be set up that will correspond with the entrants' race numbers—find yours. Once there, organize your bike gear. Lay down a towel and place on it your bike shoes or cleats (unless you have them attached to your clipless pedals), your shirt, and race belt (with your race number attached to either). Then hang your helmet and sunglasses on your bike frame, and check that your water-bottles are full.

Next, give your bike a final inspection—check the tire pressure and brakes. Then test ride the bike and put it in the gear that you want to use when you first start out of the area. Make sure that you've got everything you need: tire repair tools and a tube, a frame pump or air cannisters, and your cyclometer (cleared and set). Finally, rack your bike, and stop and get your bearings. Pick a nearby landmark and use it as a guidepost for locating your bike after the swim.

Next, set up your transition area for the run. Set the gear in the order that you are going to put it on—socks (optional), running shoes, a visor or hat, and any personal items such as sunscreen. You're now done, unless the transition areas are in two different locations. In that case, set each up with its own towels and gear arrangements.

Walk over to the finish of the swim and look at the set-up. Memorize what the exit looks like, including its terrain and footing, then look back at your bike and visualize how you will walk/run to get to your bike at the end of the swim (many triathletes forget where they have racked their bikes and waste time searching, since they didn't set a guidepost). Don't neglect to walk over to the start of the swim and select markers, such as buildings or trees, that you can use as sighting points during the swim, because it's almost impossible to ever swim in a straight line. Finally, walk over to the exit of the bike course as well, so that you are familiar with the exit and entry set-up.

The Swim

The announcer will call you to the starting line.

Although this is not the case for smaller-scale triathlons, where everyone begins together, in many larger or more sophisticated events you will begin the race in "waves." Waves are groups of individuals who are in the same age division; they usually start with two to five minute delays in between. Stand with the individuals who are marked with the same age-division letter as you.

As the starting signal sounds for your wave, enter the water with measured caution. After a few strokes, stop if you want, and take a few extra breaths. After you round the first buoy, take the time to get your bearings, breaststroke for a few yards if you have to, and remember to breathe.

As you round the last buoy and head back, do a mental body check—survey your body and scan your energy level. Go ahead and swim as close to the finish as you can, before you stand.

Swim-to-Bike Transition

This transition actually starts about 100 yards from the finish of the swim, because it's then that you'll begin to visualize the swim finish line. As you reach the shore and put your feet

Fernanda Keller quickly strips off her wetsuit in the Danskin Women's Triathlon Series swim-to-bike transition area.

down, you might feel dizzy—most of us do. Your equilibrium may be thrown off by coming from a prone to an upright position, but you'll regain it quickly. There may be volunteers in the water to help you; listen to their instructions, and take care to drink at the aid station.

In a controlled fashion, walk or run through the flagged area that has been constructed for a finishing shoot and find your bike rack. If you are wearing a wetsuit, strip it off. Stand and slip on your bike shoes or cleats, your race number and/or shirt, your sunglasses, and helmet (it must be buckled). Then take your bike off the rack, start your cyclometer, and either ride or walk the bike out of the transition area, whichever is required. The less time you spend in transition, the faster your finishing time.

Some of you may decide to change your clothes for each of the three events. I don't recommend it, but there are usually changing corrals or tents for this purpose. To avoid the time-consuming process of clothes-changing, I suggest you swim in a lycra suit, then slip on a pair of cycling or fitness shorts, and leave them on for the run. You can wear a singlet or shirt for the run as well, but don't wear it on the bike unless it is cold, because the shirt will create greater wind resistance.

Enjoy the ride.

The Bike

I love the start of the bicycle leg. I am fresh, happy, and excited. What I need to do at that point is relax and ride according to my pre-race strategy—at a set speed, not at the pace that my heart is going.

As you start, remind yourself not to draft and remember to talk to riders as you approach them, shouting out that you are passing. Always try to pass to the left, but don't ever cross the center line of the road.

You should start drinking almost immediately from your water-bottle, and, if the bike portion is over 25 miles, you may need to eat during the ride, as well.

As you near the second transition, remember to go slowly through the chicane (the traffic cones that are set up to slow you down as you ride into or out of a transition area), and ride with extra care in the transition area, because runners will be exiting down the corridors between the bike racks.

Bike-to-Run Transition

Again, the transition starts about a half-mile from the finish of the bike leg, when you start to prepare mentally for the run. Drink as much fluid as you possibly can at this point, so that you are hydrated for the run start.

Once into the transition area, find the place that is assigned for your bike and rack it. Unbuckle your helmet *after* you get off the bike (that's a Tri-Fed/USA rule). Slip off your bike shoes, slide on your racing flats, put on a visor, add a shirt if you want one, and take off.

The Run

Immediately you will feel an entirely new sensation in your legs, what triathletes call "the grip." The changeover from cycling muscles (those in the front of the thigh—the quadriceps) to running muscles (those located in the back of the thigh—the

Former world champion body builder Carla Dunlap (left) standing at the finish of her first triathlon with fellow competitor Leah Morris. There are too few black women today in triathlon.

hamstrings) results in an incredible tightening. You will notice that you can't extend your legs as far as you would like and that your stride frequency (turnover rate) is impaired. It usually takes from several hundred yards to as much as a couple of miles before your legs recover from the triathlon grip, but eventually you'll settle in to your chosen pace.

Other runners will pass you, just as swimmers and cyclists have done. You will pass other runners as well. Those with strong backgrounds in all three rarely get passed. Balance is the solution to winning in this sport.

As you approach the final finish line, look up—there will be a finish clock with the time. It's guaranteed to display the wrong time, because it will be measuring the time from the first wave, and you are probably in one of the later ones. Remember the time, though; you can subtract out your wave handicap when you are thinking more clearly. Or, better still, look at your wristwatch—it is best to rely on your own timing, anyway.

Finally, throw your shoulders back, hold your head up, and run across the finish line—you are not only a triathlete, you are a finisher!

The most vivid highlights of my athletic career have occurred at the finish line of races. Running towards the finish banner, with the spectators applauding, the announcer saying my name over the loudspeaker, and looking up at a finish clock that reads the numbers that match my goal is pure exhilaration. I have one overriding thought that always hits me at that moment. I think that if I had just known how good the finish-line experience would be, I would have trained more.

That feeling of awakening takes me around again to a new beginning, because with every ending there is the opportunity for a new start. That *is* racing.

The start of one of the Danskin Women's Triathlon Series races.

9

Triathletic Health

I have often said that just being "healthy" is an inferior state to being *fit*, and it is, because health is simply the absence of injury and disease. Fitness is a step above health and is the ability to perform physically. You can be healthy and not fit. You cannot be fit and not healthy. None of this means that your health is unimportant, however; your good health is a necessary prerequisite to your fitness. So, keeping in mind our "big" goal of fitness, let's look at a small but literally vital goal, *health*.

Nutrition

The first component of health is proper nutrition, and the cornerstone of proper nutrition (and lifetime weight control) is the achievement of a balance between the calories you put into your body (by eating) and the calories you put out (through training or exercise).

I suggest that the calories you put into your body consist of 60% carbohydrates, in order for your body to have sufficient glycogen (produced from the breakdown of carbohydrates) to move your muscles; 25% fat, providing the fatty acids and triglycerides which are necessary for activity and the processes of metabolism; and 15% protein, which contains plenty of amino acids for your body to use in rebuilding your cells.

On the "calories out" side of the fitness equation, I suggest that you stick to your personal training program, dutifully and joyfully. Exercise affects every cell of your body, making calorie burning more efficient for the following reasons:

- Exercise increases the size and number of your body's mitochondria (these are tiny energy "factories" which use oxygen to transform food into energy—the process known as metabolism), resulting in an increase of your body's ability to burn fat fuel.

- Exercise increases, by up to 80 percent, the amount of oxygen delivered to the muscles.

- Exercise increases your heart's size, resulting in greater stroke volume, each heartbeat pushing out a greater amount of blood.

- Exercise shifts your body's tissue composition, changing fat to muscle, with the resulting muscle tissue burning more calories than the previous fatty tissue.

Injuries and Accidents

The second component of health is the avoidance (or treatment) of injuries. Triathlon can be a dangerous sport. Once I was being treated for lacerations and abrasions from a bike wreck in the medical tent at the Bud Light USTS-Baltimore. Scott Molina was nearby, and I overheard him in a moment of utter exasperation releasing a few choice expletives regarding the bike leg of the event. The bike course was on the streets of the city, through major intersections that were closed to traffic. He had been in the lead, spinning through the streets at high speed, trusting that the course marshals had stopped all vehicles. However, just as Molina entered one intersection, a fire truck also sped through from the other direction, responding to an emergency. The two missed by an inch.

It rattled him for a long time.

Tri-training can actually help you avoid many of the overuse injuries that plague single-sport specialists, because you alternate muscle groups in your workouts. However, triathletes also have to be wary of three times as many injuries as do single-sport athletes—we can get a swimmer's shoulder, cyclist's knees, *and* runner's feet.

The most common injuries are the result of overuse and are generally of one of two types: stress fractures or inflammation (of the tendons, ligaments, bursa, cartilage, connective tissues, or nerve tissues).

All overuse injuries share the same common causes—repeated stress on a given structure that overwhelms its capacity to respond and repair itself. Or, quite simply, repetitive trauma from training errors.

Among runners, the most common cause of problems is excessive mileage or the over-training syndrome. Other causes are also in the too-much or too-soon categories:

- too fast an increase in the distances in your training schedule;
- too much of an increase in resistance training, such as climbing hills;
- too much interval training, too soon;
- too many or too intense bounding or jumping exercises;
- too much time spent running on hard surfaces.

Other injuries are caused by training errors, such as training in the wrong shoes, inadequate stretching/warming up, lack of adequate flexibility and/or strength, imbalanced muscle development, and uncompensated leg-length differences.

Injuries are common in both sexes and have been found to be more sport-specific than sex-specific. There are some indications that women may have a higher overall incidence of injury, but the injury patterns are the same. Women do appear to have a higher incidence of shin splints and stress fractures, but they also seem to have a lower incidence of certain types of tendonitis.

When I competed in the 1984 U.S. Olympic Marathon Trials, my competition and I were surveyed, and researchers found that a very high number (44 percent) of the 210 women reported that they had suffered from a musculoskeletal problem that they considered significant. Of those who qualified for the trials, 10 percent were unable to compete because they were injured at the time of the race.

Are women more at risk of overuse injuries than men?

It appears that there is a higher rate of injury among female athletes, but that it is predominantly caused by their lower initial levels of fitness. As women become more active and competitive, their rates of injury approach those of men.

Most people believe that women suffer from more knee

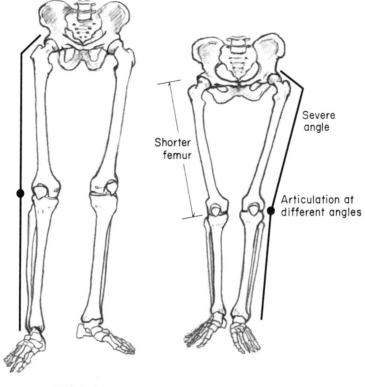

Male Pelvis   *Female Pelvis*

problems than men, because of the wider female pelvis and greater joint flexibility. In fact, knee pain among runners is the most common injury for both sexes, occurring in 24 percent of the men and 27 percent of the women runners, which is not a big difference.

It appears that women suffer from more stress fractures than men, but some specific stress fractures may occur less often in women. It is reported that stress fractures of the iliac crest (the bone you feel when you put your hands on your hips) and the tarsal navicular (one of the bones in the middle and inside of the foot) are more predominant among men. Again, the increased rate of stress fractures, similar to other overuse injuries, is likely to be related to the initial lack of proper conditioning.

There are other orthopedic stress traumas. The incidence of swimmer's shoulder (pain from repeated trauma to the

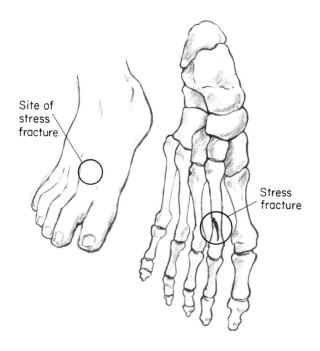

Site of stress fracture

Stress fracture

Tarsal navicular stress-fracture

head of the upper arm bone) is higher among women (reported by 68 percent, versus 50 percent of men).

The most common problem for swimmers are ear infections, which are totally non-gender dependent. Ear infections are caused by exposure of the tissues in the ear canal to prolonged irrigation. The best treatment is prevention—wearing ear plugs and thoroughly drying the ears (there are chemicals that can do this). Once symptoms are present, you must decrease the inflammation and simultaneously treat the infection.

Treatment

As far as overuse injuries go, rest is the best treatment. However, if your condition is serious, then casting, crutches, anti-inflammatory drugs, or physical therapy may be required. For non-serious injuries, treating the problem yourself first, by using rest, ice, compression, and elevating the injured part is an OK option.

Diagnose the pain. You can't keep a problem from recurring if you don't know its cause. Every overuse injury is

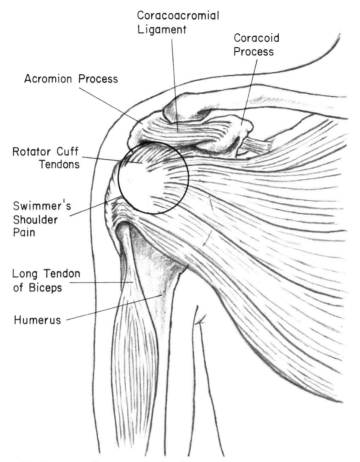

Coracoacromial
Ligament

Coracoid
Process

Acromion Process

Rotator Cuff
Tendons

Swimmer's
Shoulder
Pain

Long Tendon
of Biceps

Humerus

The location of "swimmers shoulder"—a common injury point.

caused by a force on a tissue that is greater than the tissue's
basic strength, and every injury-causing force can be traced to
one of the following causes:

- training errors that do not allow for adequate recovery;
- tissues that are weak and susceptible to injury;
- biomechanical weaknesses that put excessive stress on certain parts of your body.

When you know what caused it, you can begin to fix it.

Rehabilitation, using flexibility, strengthening, and aerobic/anaerobic conditioning, is the key to returning to your training program. If you are injured, cross-train in a different sport that doesn't hurt, until the pain disappears. If you continue to train with pain, you only exacerbate the problem and delay healing.

Common Discomforts

There are a number of minor discomforts that are associated with any exercise program. The thing to remember about all of them is that they are your body's way of letting you know that something is slightly out of balance. Being tough and ignoring pain is not a particularly wise move, because willful ignorance can turn a minor problem into a major one.

Side aches. Side aches or "stitches" generally seem to be caused by overexertion. The exact cause of side aches is unknown, but it is suspected that gas caught in the upper intestines might be a frequent culprit. There are a few tricks that sometimes work to stop the pain:

- put pressure from your fingers directly on the place that hurts;
- massage the general area with your whole hand;
- straighten your back and stretch tall;
- relax your breathing and slow down the number of breaths you are taking per minute;
- lean forward, bending at the waist.

Post-workout nausea. Variously, this can be caused from eating too much just before a workout, or from not eating enough, so that your body doesn't have enough easily accessible calories with which to work. Nausea can also be caused by dehydration. Experiment with your drinking and eating patterns and see what helps.

Blisters. They can be caused by shoes and/or socks that don't fit well, that have tight spots, or are wet. Small blisters can be covered with medicated cream and a bandage. Large blisters should be drained with a sterilized needle, then treated with medicated cream and a covering. Pay attention to them—they can get infected.

Muscle cramps. What feels like painful knots are actually involuntary contractions of the muscle. It is not known what causes them—it could be a lack of sodium, potassium, calcium, or a vitamin complex. To help get rid of the pain, stretch the joint, massage the area, and "walk it off" by gently moving the muscle. Then look at your diet, and if cramps happen frequently, change your drinking and eating habits and see if that helps.

Illness

It's a tough call—whether or not to exercise when you are sick or not. But it's probably better to be safe than sorry, so it's generally not a bad idea to take a few days off when your immune system is impaired by illness. If you must continue to train when you are ill, reduce the amount and intensity.

For a cold, if you can take a few days off, do so. There is no proof that complete bed rest cures virus colds any faster than not resting, nor is there any proof that training extends the duration of a cold, but do play it safe.

If you have a fever, don't work out. Your heart is already doing double time by maintaining metabolic function as well as pumping blood to the skin's surface in order to reduce the heat from the fever. Don't add a third load on your system.

Gynecological Concerns

The past two decades have brought hundreds of thousands of women into the world of exercise and athletic training. The medical experts have given them the green light—regular exercise can only improve the quality of women's lives. That's a fact.

Here are some of the conditions that can affect any woman, athletic or not, and the facts that relate to them with regards to the impact of training.

Vaginitis. Training itself does not cause vaginitis, nor does it cure it. However, wearing non-breathable training apparel can cause a moister than normal vaginal environment, which can encourage the overgrowth of yeast, the major cause of vaginitis. If you have a recurring problem with vaginitis (or even if you don't), it would not be a bad idea to always wear training apparel made of breathable fabrics, such as cotton or rayon blends. In any case, if you notice the onset of vaginitis (the common symptoms are discharge, itching, odor, and discomfort), consult your gynecologist, who will treat it with appropriate medication.

Stress Urinary Incontinence. This is a condition of

involuntary urine leakage, which occurs when there is an increase in abdominal pressure such as from jumping, running, or straining. It is not directly caused by sports activities and is usually found in women who have given birth several times. Training can cause an increase in abdominal pressure and, as a result, involuntary leakage symptoms, but exercise does not worsen a condition which is already present. Consult a urologist to determine the cause. To aid with the problem, empty your bladder before you train, follow specific exercises that can strengthen the muscles involved, and wear a mini-pad. Don't let this problem stop you from training.

Contraception. It's your call. Your decision on which type of contraceptive agent to use is not affected by the fact that you train. The decision is based solely on your choice of a safe and effective way of preventing conception.

Menstrual Irregularity. Any woman who has irregular menstrual cycles should consult a gynecologist to determine the cause. Irregular periods or amenorrhea is indeed more common among athletically active women than sedentary women, but it is not known why. *Athletic amenorrhea* is a condition of menstrual irregularity caused by exercise. Amenorrhea may be caused by the physical stress of training, the emotional stress of competition, hormonal changes, loss of body weight due to increased physical activity, or a change in eating patterns. However, recent studies indicate that athletic amenorrhea may be primarily caused by eating disorders, not exercise, so don't stop training, and don't stop eating.

If you experience frequent, prolonged, heavy, or unexpected menstrual periods and there are no associated gynecological problems, it is not recommended that you try to manipulate your periods using hormones. Menstruation is an inconvenience, but there's nothing to do but accept it—that's one of the prices you pay for being a woman.

It appears that in athletic amenorrheic women, normal periods resume once training is reduced. Likewise, fertility is restored to normal upon resumption of a normal menstrual cycle.

Menstrual Cramps. Other costs of womanhood, premenstrual and menstrual discomfort, are usually reduced by training. These strong and intermittent lower abdominal pains do not preclude you from working out. It's perfectly safe to exercise at all times during the month. If menstrual cramps are frequently or regularly severe or debilitating, consult your gynecologist and try to keep training.

Pregnancy. One of your greatest athletic achievements may be getting fit before getting pregnant and staying fit during pregnancy. If it isn't your greatest athletic achievement, it can still be one of your life's high times.

Even though physical conditioning is certainly good for pregnant women, there are certain precautions that must be followed. Training vigorously can result in excessive heat (hyperthermia), lowered oxygen supply that could reduce that of the fetus, inadequate blood flow, or abdominal traumas.

A program of general conditioning is desirable for moms-to-be; your pregnancy, labor, and delivery will all likely be easier for your efforts. However, always check with your obstetrician before starting or continuing a vigorous conditioning program. If you weren't training before the pregnancy, once pregnant you shouldn't start up a program any more strenuous than walking. Weight training, stretching, and calisthenics are good conditioning activities for pregnant women.

Varicose Veins. The enlarged veins that appear near the skin's surface are not caused by exercise, but by malfunctioning blood vessel valves. Exercise not only helps relieve the pain from varicose veins, but it can also help treat the condition. Do not confuse athletic veins with varicose veins. Some athletes have large veins because of their bodies' need to carry larger amounts of blood to the skin's surface for its thermoregulatory (cooling) effects.

Anemia. Not an uncommon affliction of female athletes, anemia is a disease characterized by an abnormally low number of red blood cells (RBC), and it is usually caused by the loss of iron that occurs in menstruation, or by not eating sufficient iron-rich foods. Sometimes because of the effects of heavy training, there can be a loss of iron through the intestines and in your stools. "Athletic anemia" is a condition of low red blood cell count that is due to an increase in the volume of blood without a corresponding increase in the number of cells. It is not real anemia, it is just that when training, your blood volume may increase as much as 10 percent faster than your RBC concentration.

For whichever cause, one out of every four women in America is iron deficient, and one out of 20 is anemic. To be iron deficient means that your iron reserves (iron that is stored in your liver, spleen, bone marrow, and other tissues) are low. Once your iron stores are used up, you become anemic. The average-sized woman can buy insurance against iron deficiency by taking three 100-gram iron tablets each week.

Additional Help

If you would like to connect with key women's health resources and research organizations in the United States, you can contact the following groups:

Melpomene Institute for Women's Health Research
1010 University Avenue
St. Paul, MN 55104
(612) 378-0545
Membership Costs: $25 per year with a newsletter

The Melpomene Institute identifies and researches health issues important to physically active women. Access to this information is provided through their Resource Center, information packets, brochures, and talks.

The Women's Sports Foundation
342 Madison Ave., Suite 728
New York, NY 10173
(800) 227-3988
(212) 972-9170
Membership Costs: $15-100, includes a quarterly
newsletter

The Women's Sports Foundation is dedicated to promoting the participation of women in sports activities. The WSF is a non-profit foundation that supports individual athletes and programs through grants, maintains a toll-free telephone number for referrals and education, and is the advocacy organization for women's sports. As a trustee of the Foundation, I urge you to join and support this important cause.

Safety

Women are prime targets for physical abuse in any of its forms—your responsiblity (and it's unfortunate that you have to do this) is to reduce the chances of being a target.

Here are 15 rules of safety for all triathletic women. Think about each one as you read them and ask yourself, "Do I do that?" Then, add these safety rules as key ingredients in your training regimen.

Remember to follow all 15 of them—they are so important that you should think of them as laws, not rules.

#1. Avoid Habits. It may seem logical to always run or ride at the same time of day, on the same course, in the same way, but don't. An assailant will often plan their attack, so vary your patterns and never allow them that opportunity.

#2. Never Travel Alone. Train in twos. You are safest when there is someone else with you. Recently, I had an accident—I tripped while running alone and broke my ankle. The damage from walking home and dragging my bad foot caused months of delay in my recovery and left me an easy target.

#3. Trust Nothing. Don't ever trust that you are perfectly safe, because you aren't. Don't block your senses while out training, such as by wearing headphones. It's vital that you are able to see and hear what is going on around you.

Never traveling alone is one of the safety principles of training. Here Sylviane and Patricia Puntous, former Ironwomen winners of the Ironman and two identical twins, wait together for the pro women's wave to start.

#4. Beware of the Night. Wear reflective gear whenever the lighting is insufficient: nights, early mornings, in fog or inclement weather. Purchase reflective patches and stick them on your shoes, your hat, everywhere, and always try to train in well-lit areas.

#5. Practice Prevention. Always be prepared for the worst case scenario—carry a coin to make a pay telephone call, have identification on you when you are out on the roads, tell someone where you are going before you leave. An ounce of prevention may be worth your life.

#6. Be Aware that Trouble Can Come Anytime, from Anybody. Attacks happen any time of day and are committed by anyone. There is no average profile of an assailant—the only common denominator is that they are always male. And just because a stranger is dressed in a three-piece suit doesn't mean he isn't a rapist—they are getting more sophisticated.

#7. Know Your Turf. Know the area in which you swim, bike, and run, and become familiar with some of the folks along the way. Know where there are police call boxes or telephones, and recognize where there is dense foliage or places for attackers to hide.

#8. Have a Plan. Make a decision about what you are going to do in different circumstances. For example, if someone enters your "safety zone," that personal space which strangers may not violate, move away quickly.

#9. Don't Assume Anything. Just because you have ridden a certain course for years doesn't mean that it's going to be safe tomorrow. A local inhabitant might have just adopted a stray dog that likes to attack cyclists.

#10. Use Anger. Anger may be your best weapon, because it can intimidate, buy you precious time, and give a potential attacker second thoughts. You may even have to use profanity in your anger, and I believe that God will forgive you if you have to curse to stay alive.

#11. Use Something. Carry a whistle, a can of mace, or car keys—something so that if you have to fight, you have more than your hands and feet for weapons.

#12. Don't Talk with or Stop for Strangers. It's a rule you learned as a child, but may have dismissed as an adult— don't strike up a conversation unless you know the other person. If verbally harassed, ignore the individual involved. If followed, stopping and staring at the person will let them know that you are not unaware and they are not unseen.

#13. Don't Be Dumb. Don't wear expensive jewelry or watches when you train—it's amazing what people will do to take them from you. The less you have the less they will want to take.

#14. If They are Armed, You Are Supposed to Give It to Them. If it's a material item, by all means give it to an armed robber. If they want to rape you, there is no "best" solution. When I was in Viet Nam during the war, an American GI attempted to rape one of my fellow Red Cross members who was sleeping in the quarters several doors away. She feigned an epileptic attack, and he left.

#15. Turn Them In. If you are attacked, memorize everything—his face, size, clothes, anything unusual. Call the police as soon as possible, and do everything you can to help the police find him.

Physical violation is a form of terrorism that you may experience in your lifetime—eight out of every 10 women do. Within a thousandth of a second, you are going to have to respond and make the right decision or pay a huge price. Some attackers are discouraged by anger, but flight might be more effective than fighting with others. In any case, the best cure for this particular illness, violence, is prevention. So don't be dumb, and do play by these rules of safety.

10

Matters of the Head and Heart

"If you, Sally, can run a hundred miles, finish a dozen Ironmans, qualify for the Olympic Marathon Trials, run a business, write a half-dozen books, and stand up in front of an audience of one thousand and speak, then I can start a training program," a customer recently told me when I asked her why she wanted to buy a pair of Nike Air cross-trainers.

I responded by asking her what she wanted to *train for.*

She answered, "I want to train in order to change my life."

What a goal—to change your life. Standing next to me was a middle-aged woman who was taking those first few difficult steps, working towards making that difference in her life. It isn't going to be easy for her, but anything that is easy is probably not worth doing.

Training For Enjoyment

Triathletes are tatooed as pain-seeking athletes—the toughest of them all. I am always amazed when people ask me the "who" question, because when I answer that "I am a triathlete," a look of reverence appears. That didn't occur when I used to say that I was an ultra-marathoner who won hundred-mile races, in my pre-triathlon athletic era.

Two Japanese competitors finishing Ironman-Japan with the broad smile of victory.

That triathletes eat nails and only know how to talk to a bike, their running sneakers, or themselves as they float, coast, and shuffle is a myth.

We are really simple folks. We train because we have fun at it, certainly not for the money or the fame, and usually not because of our egos. When I tell people that I have fun when I train, they again scrunch their faces into a look of incredulity. For me, training for triathlons really is a matter of having fun and being a kid again. The three skills of triathlon are really those of pre-adolescence—swimming, cycling, and running are all kids' activities—and now as a grown-up it is acceptable for me to play in their playground again.

"Can it really be fun to train for two or three hours a day?" they ask. For me it's the truth—training *is* the best part of my day. When I train, I don't have to make business decisions about hiring and firing; I don't have to use money shopping or paying bills; I don't have to stay in one place, like at a desk or a home; and I don't have to get bored by the grind. When I train, I let my mind go as much as I do my body. I have some of my most creative moments when I am training, and I am never bored (although I do get tired).

Triathlons really are for fun.

Icebergs

It was said well in 1952:

"Not to have confidence in one's own body is to lose confidence in oneself...It is precisely the female athletes, who, being positively interested in their own game, feel themselves less handicapped in comparison with the male."
Simone de Beauvoir, *The Second Sex*

Most of us want to be feminine. Most of us want to be athletes. Somewhere between the two there is a problem: we feel we can't be both, because the two are such opposites that one must suffer for the other. We want to be athletes, which requires that we be tough, aggressive, and forceful, even dominant. But we must submerge our athletic side when we want to be feminine, a role which is understood to be supportive, passive, tender, emotional. What is a woman supposed to be and do?

It's the same problem I have as an Ironwoman competing in the Ironman. All of the T-shirts, award plaques, and prize money paychecks that I ever receive read "Ironman," and yet that's not me. There is a large amount of what sports psychologists call "role conflict" involved with being a woman and being called an Ironman.

Women often react to this confusion in one of two ways. On the one hand, there are female Ironman winners who wear jewelry, two-piece, high-cut swimsuits for all three events, and cross the finish line with a feminine glow. On the other side, there are women who win the Ironman decked out in the highest-tech gear and apparel, which makes them so fast that when they cross the finish line they have reached total, unglamorous exhaustion.

My resolution of this role conflict and its resultant confusion, what I call the "iceberg complex," is to work on the thawing principle. The woman with the skimpy two-piece and the woman with the high-tech apparatus are just acting out the two thawing ends of an iceberg. One doesn't want to be perceived as too tough and the other as too feminine, and neither as androgynous. Both choices are equally valid, and there is room for both models of women in athletics today, whereas, 30 or 40 years ago, there was room for neither. Indeed there are clear signs of improvement—the Women's Sports Foundation performed research in 1988 which showed that 87 percent of today's moms and dads accept the idea that sports are equally important for boys and girls.

Yet the media still hangs on to the need for women to fit a mold. When a local newspaper recently interviewed a female pro triathlete, the journalist wrote, "Jan Ripple, mother of three, and her husband...," with the underlying meaning that even though she is an athlete, she is still fulfilling her primary roles of wife and mother. Never have I read, "Scott Molina, husband and father of one..." As the iceberg thaws, the traditional notion of the female as someone's spouse, mother, or daughter dwindles—she, you, and I become who we really are, sportswomen.

I can hardly wait for it to melt, and it better happen in my lifetime.

Relationships

As the offspring of the running revolution, the sport of triathlon watched hordes of runners and marathoners learn to cope with their new lifestye—fitting together a training regimen with other interpersonal commitments. The relationship statistics from the running population during the 1980s were brutal:

- the divorce rate was three times higher among runners than the national average;
- male runners married to sedentary females had only a 50-50 chance of overcoming marital difficulties, while marriages of female runners to sedentary men fared even more poorly. (Interestingly, female runners were twice as likely as male runners to reassess their relationships due to sports.)

There are complicated reasons why running may lead to marital and relationship problems, reasons that extend beyond the mere time spent pounding roads and trails. And triathlon, as running's stepchild, is similar enough for me to wonder whether it, too, produces noticeable strains on relationships.

There are certainly aspects of triathlon that could contribute to the decay of personal relationships. Triathlon, like running, is a solitary endeavor that can become both self-absorbing and narcissistic. These are also both sports where, even if both partners participate, they are usually excluded from one another's presence.

Finally, the athletic turf is one of the last male bastions for identity and power. So when a woman beats a man at his own game, the true test of equality and acceptance begins.

Training also leads to enhanced self-confidence. This new esteem can lead to questioning one's choices, among them, whether or not to proceed with a marriage or have children.

Finally, I can't deny that training takes time. The time it takes to train is sometimes the same time that a triathlete would have spent with friends and family. Sadly, the competition for time can be such a fierce battle that when the dust settles there may not be a relationship.

On the other hand, there are aspects of triathlon that can contribute to the growth of personal relationships. Training can lead to stability, commitment, discipline and tenacity, and getting in shape often results in increased emotional stability, toughness, and flexibility.

Without a doubt, training alone has never made or broken a marriage or a relationship or divided a family. However, if training becomes an obsession and dominates life to the exclusion of all else, then it's time to do some self-analysis, in order to find out what has driven you to such an extreme. Sports should enhance your life, providing you with the riches

The Run-Jump-Climb kids triathlon at the Danskin Women's Triathlon. The key feature of every event is to include the entire family in the sport (and to start them at a young age—this was the starting wave for the 2–3 year olds).

of health and experience, but it is a monster if it controls you.

The sharing of a lifestyle that includes athletic participation is central to the success of any relationship between athletes over the long run, swim, or bike. Triathlons may strain a healthy relationship, just as they strain a healthy heart—for the *good!*

A Special Note to Tri-Parents

After childbirth, tri-fitness is redefined. Luckily, you're the one who gets to write the new definition of your own fitness, so you can either give up training and wallow in soap operas and chocolate or become very creative about training.

Assuming you select the latter, here are a few creative ideas:

(1) Get the right equipment to train: You need to invest in a Baby Jogger for running, backpacks for walking, and bike trailers for cycling.

(2) Get a training partner and alternate training times: Find another parent as your training partner. While one parent is out, the other watches the children. The children love it,

because they are outdoors and they learn the exercise routine (which equates with play to them). If you can't find a fellow parent-training partner, advertise for one in a local running or cycling newsletter.

(3) Join a club that provides childcare: At many athletic clubs, childcare is available. Check before you join.

(4) Enroll your children in sports programs: At the same time your kids are training with their soccer, swim, or softball teams, you, too, can train.

Getting Older and Better

Undoubtedly, women (and men) experience major physical changes that affect their athletic performance as they become older. One of my training partners, Gabrielle Anderson-Scheiss, a 1984 Olympian, and I have teamed up several times to compete in and win the Levi Ride-and-Tie, a race that includes two runners and one horse. We were both beyond the age of 40 when we most recently won the race as a team.

Both of us have raced for several decades and have long been curious about the cumulative effects of hard athletic training on our racing performances. When I recently asked her how she was doing, she said, "I can run as fast as ever but I can't recover as quickly as before." And I, after 10 years of racing as an Ironwoman in Ironmans, this year set a personal best time of 10 hours and 42 minutes, 15 minutes faster than I have ever raced before. I am getting older *and* better, but I, too, have noticed a slowing in my recovery time.

There is no question that getting faster doesn't go on forever. Yet the midpoint in life, formerly around the age of 40, is being pushed further towards the age of 50 as we live active lifestyles in healthy environments, supported by proper food and medical care. But, on the average, at the age of fifty (actually, in the Western world, it is 51 years), women begin menopause.

Menopause is a natural phenomenon—menstruation stops and your hormone levels change. There are certain accompanying changes as well, one of which may be osteoporosis, the loss of bone density. Still, there is a good deal that can be done to allay this condition—there are certain exercises (weight-bearing activities such as running are highly beneficial), nutritional supplements, and lifestyle changes that can prevent significant bone loss. Training can also reduce the symptoms of

Pointing out that getting older means doing it better, Sally Edwards, 44 years old, at the Danskin Women's Triathlon.

depression, insomnia, and anxiety that are associated with menopause.

Once you hit menopause, you are going to be forced to make a decision on hormone replacement therapies, as well. A woman whom I admire for her commitment to a lifetime of training and racing recently said to me, "I want more research on the effects of aging on athletic women—I have read everything I can find and there is little really known about the influ-

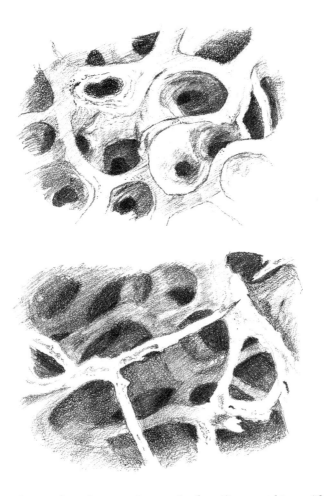

Artist's rendering of an electron micrograph of an iliac crest biopsy. The upper drawing shows bone from a normal subject; the lower shows the thinning and breakup of trabecular plates in a woman with osteoporosis..

ences of hormone replacement on the effects of aging in women and on most parameters of athletics."

She's right.

It is known that after the onset of menopause, women tend to have higher cholesterol levels and proportional drops in the "good" type of cholesterol (known as "HDL") in their bloodstreams, and both these symptoms are risk factors of heart disease. On the positive side, it has also been shown that physical training programs can result in a relative increase of HDL levels, as well as lowering cholesterol levels overall.

For those who are past their midpoint and considering starting a triathlon program, I urge you to begin. Not only are the psychological, physiological, and social benefits important, but just the excitement of a new challenge can make it worth your while to take the triathlon adventure ride.

You're never too old to start something new. Even though some people retire from life at age 50 and hide in a recliner, why should you?

For me, aging is a secret athletic weapon, because each year I understand so much more about (and learn so much more from) the sport experience. If you ask me why I set a personal best time at the Japan Ironman last year, I would tell you it's because I now know what it takes to excel, like I have never known before. It wasn't my heart and lungs that made it possible; it was being the best at who I am—a triathlete and a woman.

About Men

It's tough to break with tradition; some people never can.

In my case, I was taught like my mother to grow up, marry, have 2.2 children and live happily ever after. However, thanks to my military-officer father, who raised my three older brothers to be athletes and soldiers, I was also reared as an athlete, because my dad just didn't know any other approach.

It's not hard to understand why more of my fellow athletic sisters aren't lining up at the starting line with me. In my age group, masters women (women 40 years of age and older), the majority of females weren't given even the mixed support as children that I had. According to Marsha Smelkinson, marketing director for the Bud Light Triathlon Series, only 1.1 percent of participants at the BLTS are women 40 to 44 years of age.

I must thank each of those masters women for being there. I know what it takes to run against the tide, against the peer-group pressure that requires conformity. I know just how hard it is to stand on a beach beside larger and stronger males, scantily clad in your swimsuit. But, with each passing event, we continue to dispel the outmoded tradition of "a woman's place is..." (you can fill in the rest).

In my first book on triathlons, I wanted to open with a discussion of the real problem for most female triathletes—fear, stemming from intimidation. My editor argued that men couldn't imagine the fear that comes from standing next to people who are a minimum of 4 inches taller than you and 40 pounds heavier. Men, he said, could only fear the race, not the racers.

Men, as a sex, view women's lack of participation differently than do women. Many believe that since women are not as strong or as fast, since they don't beat men's times, their performance is less important. Men have grown accustomed to (and some prefer) women serving as the support team, in the home and on the playgrounds of triathlon. For them, the woman's place is understood to be behind her man, her athlete. Any other place, such as biking down the road in front of him, may be threatening. Competition or discouragement from their significant others is but one of women's barriers to participation.

Do race promoters and the media take women as seriously as they do men? Let's look at the facts. In races, women start in waves behind the men. They frequently receive smaller and fewer trophies, and the winners on the awards stage who receive the loudest applause and the most attention are always the top finishers in the men's division. Finally, the photos in the newspaper the next day invariably show the men's winner breaking the tape. If there is a picture of the women's winner, it is typically buried in the back of the article, just as women's results are.

Women themselves can create barriers to their own participation. Many potential female competitors are *at* races, but they stand on the sidelines as spectators. They watch us, and I wonder what they're thinking. The female spectator dishes out her own brand of peer pressure—she comes to the race to support her man. She helps carry the gear and the kids, takes pictures at the finish line and brings the post-race food and drinks. She is ready to give the massages, and in return, she receives laurels of praise for her support.

She isn't confused like the female athlete who bears the

dual roles of being "feminine" and being strong and sweaty. The female athlete takes the risk of racing to the finish line and arriving there looking disheveled and exhausted. And who is there to support her, to bring the kids and the camera, waiting for her to finish?

A woman's real place is wherever she wants it to be, and it is time for everyone to recognize that women's reasons for not being triathletes are different from men's reasons. And it is time to support those women who want to tear down the wall of sexist tradition.

Hopefully, in the future it won't take a father like mine, who raised his daughter as his fourth son, for a little girl to grow into a triathletic woman.

Men can have a great deal to do with that change.

The Future for Women in Triathlon

Nearly a decade ago, I wrote the first book ever published on our sport, *Triathlons: A Triple Fitness Sport*. In that book, I made some predictions on the future of the young event:

- triathlon will become an Olympic sport;
- triathlon will take on global importance, with an international series and prize money;
- triathlon will be viewed by the public as a true, all-around fitness contest and will generate superstars.

My predictions have come true. Hopefully, you can share my vision of what the future may hold, as I look ahead to the future of women in triathlon:

Increased Participation. Currently, triathlon races are made up of 22 percent women and 78 percent men. With the increased acceptance of women in sports and the increased opportunities available to women to be who they are, these numbers should achieve a balanced 50-50 ratio. The largest number of new participants in the single sports of swimming, cycling, and running are women, so it shouldn't be long before many make the transition to triathlon.

Equal Opportunities. Today, a professional woman triathlete makes approximately 55 cents to every dollar that her male counterpart makes—it's about the same with most professions in America. As the value of women's work is recognized

The first wave of many at the Danskin Women's Triathlon.

and the unalienable rights to equal pay for equal work are man-
dated, a woman should make a dollar for every dollar a man
makes.

* *Research.* Triathlon participation will promote research
into the areas of biological differences, physiological changes,
and the aging process, which will revolutionize the current body
of knowledge on athletic performance and women.

* *Front Covers.* A woman triathlete will grace the front
cover of *Sports Illustrated*. She has already *earned* the place-
ment. There is no further comment necessary.

* *Changes in the Household.* As women gain further
control over their lives through positive and motivating experiences such as triathlons, they will change the systems and struc-
tures in their homes.

* *Records Broken.* Throughout the next decade, new
world records will be set in all distances and for all ages of
women. The increased pressure from international competition
will force higher quality training which will result in improved
performances.

* *Equal Media Coverage.* Magazine, newspaper, and

television coverage of the sport will feature equal emphasis on both the women's and the men's races. Currently, the media sees the womens race as a subcategory of the men's, a second child.

- *Equal Respect.* If you put the male and female world triathlon champions in a room full of triathletes and asked the guests to stand in a line for whoever's autograph they wanted, the line by the woman would be short and probably predominantly male, because at this point women don't even recognize their own accomplishments. Women's achievements will come to be acknowledged as equal with men's, due to an increased understanding and respect for the differences in male and female physiology.

- *Role Models.* Women triathletes will become role models for children who admire athletes because of their accomplishments.

- *Running, Not Crawling Across the Finishline.* The era of Julie Moss and Jan Ripple dramatically crawling across the finish line is at an end. Today's triathletes train for competitions and cross the finish line standing tall, if tired.

- *A Women's National Series.* Danskin is currently sponsoring a triathlon series for women, and it or another like it will grow to cover 25 cities and several continents.

These prospects may sound like a dream, but they aren't. They can all come true if there is strong leadership and a commitment to change and progress.

I invite you to join the union of fitness triathletes and make the change happen.

The Sweet Spot

The day before the 1990 Bud Light Ironman Triathlon World Championships, I was in serious pre-race rest preparation sitting on the beaches of Kona, Hawaii. It was there that I received a telegram from a couple who are business friends of mine. Together, my friends Teresa and Mark have finished the Ironman nine times. They know what it's about. Their telegram was brief and to the point. It read: **Take No Prisoners.**

Mark and Teresa knew that for me this race was the last in a year's long trek of four Ironmans on four continents and that my goal was to set the masters records in all four. They

This is what the "sweet spot in sports" feels like—Sally Edwards smiling and knowing it is really all a matter of head and heart.

knew that in every race I came from behind and passed all of the other masters women. I knew that I would again have to catch my competition during the marathon leg of this race.

The next day, at the start of the marathon, my nemesis had a 21-minute lead, and I knew that her strength was running. I went after her, knowing that her lead was substantial.

There came a moment during the marathon when I had reached the point of absolute exhaustion—the high heat and winds had taken their toll. I knew that I had to shake the weariness; then, slowly, I felt a strange, difficult-to-explain rush of sensation—I call it the "sweet spot" in sports.

It was as if everything were coming together and the exhaustion was being let go; it was a feeling of possibility, blended with a sense of hope. I started to feel better—I picked up the pace, and I was joyfully conscious that what was happening was a rare phenomenon.

However, that sweet experience lasted only for a brief time. Then, one of my close friends and training partners came riding by on a moped—she was working as a spotter, reporting rather than racing that day. I asked her how far ahead the woman was that I wanted to beat. My friend said that she was about to finish, while I was still miles from the finish line. It hurt to hear.

Still, I took strength from my previous moments of sweetness and decided that I would give it my best, because in sports no one knows the outcome until the last competitor crosses the finish line. I also believe that in sports your competition is ultimately with yourself, a finishing clock, and of course, not with the people around you.

The masters woman ahead of me ended up beating me by nine minutes in 11 hours of racing. She took me as her prisoner. Yet I took that moment—the sweet spot—as mine. Both the victory and the defeat were what I made of them, and I left the experience with hope for the future.

A friend of mine had an even more dramatic experience which brought her to a similar point. Last summer, my friend Joyce and I were going to attend the Danskin Women's Triathlon-San Jose together. I was the national spokesperson for the series and had invited Joyce to join me. However, two weeks beforehand, Joyce was competing in a parent's relay after two of her three children had finished a swim meet. As she finished her 25-yard leg, for some unknown reason her heart stopped, and she passed out and went down in 13 feet of water.

Her husband pulled her out of the water, and a doctor at the meet immediately started CPR, yet when she arrived at the emergency room she still had not revived. Somehow and someway, though, Joyce's heart started to beat again. She was alive, though unconscious, for days.

Terry, her husband, called me and asked if I would visit with Joyce at the hospital, because she was struggling to maintain consciousness and heal. I went to the hospital, and she was unable to respond verbally to me, but her eyes showed that she was able to listen. I explained that recovering there in the hospital bed was like running a marathon, and that today she was at the one-mile mark with 25 to go. Each day she was to run one more mile, one day at a time.

We put up a poster in the hospital room and each day we marked off the miles that Joyce ran. She doesn't remember most of that today, but she has the poster and the new pair of Nikes that I gave her and that she kept near her bed throughout her hospital stay. She still has the Danskin T-shirt that I brought to her at the hospital, too, since she couldn't go to the race with me.

It has been six months. Last week, we went for a run together. Joyce told me that her doctors said she could not race competitively again for several years and that she had accepted it, that it was better to be alive than to race. She said that she wants to see her children grow up and that she wants them to have a mother. As we ran, she periodically checked her heart rate monitor and kept it at 140 beats a minute. We were quiet for a while, and then Joyce said, "But I still want to go with you to the Danskin Triathlon next year and come home with my finisher's T-shirt."

For Joyce (and me, too), sports is a way to reach sweet spots, those rare times when you are training or racing and you feel alive in every cell of your body and corner of your mind. Joyce came back to us with hope for the future, built upon the strength of her will and her desire to again experience the sweet spot in sports. I know the same strengths and desires are part of each woman, so I urge you to tap into them every day—they make life worth living.

The sweet spot is about the indomitable human spirit. For women, our spirit is expanding with the growing acceptance of females as fully capable human beings, with every right to access any avenue open to males. The Greek heroine Atlanta is an early prototype of the indomitable female. Abandoned by her father to die as a baby, because she was not born male, Atlanta survived and grew strong, athletic, and independent, besting many a potential husband in footraces, and thus staying free. Her spirit is alive in each of us, and we can use that radical spirit to break whatever bonds are holding us back, be they mental, emotional, or physical.

We must be connected to the truths and desires of our own spirits, if we are to live a life of sweet spots. And, conversely, following your sweet spots can help you find your own internal life-affirming spirit. By all means, find it and live it, and take very good care of yourself while you are doing so.

BIBLIOGRAPHY

TRIATHLON BOOKS

Allen, Mark with Bob Babbitt. *Mark Allen's Total Triathlete.* Chicago: Contemporary Books, 1988.

Baker, Erin and John Hellemans. *Triathlon: The Winning Edge.* Auckland: Heinemann Reed, 1988.

Edwards, Sally. *Triathlon Log.* Sacramento: FLEET FEET Press, 1982.

Edwards, Sally. *Triathlon: A Triple Fitness Sport.* Chicago: Contemporary Books, 1983.

Edwards, Sally. *Triathlon Training and Racing.* Chicago: Contemporary Books, 1985.

Edwards, Sally. *Triathlons for Fun.* Santa Monica: Triathlete Magazine, 1992.

Edwards, Sally. *Triathlons for Women.* Santa Monica: Triathlete Magazine, 1992.

Edwards, Sally. *Triathlons for Kids.* Santa Monica: Triathlete Magazine, 1992.

Engelhardt, Martin and Alexandra Kremer. *Triathlon: Technique, Training and Competition.* Great Britain: Springfield Books Limited, 1987.

Horning, Dave and Gerald Couzens. *Triathlon: Lifestyle of Fitness.* New York: Wallaby Books, 1985.

Lachmann, Gunter, and Thomas Steffens. *Triathlon: Die Krone der Ausdauer.* Hilden: Spirodon, 1983. (German)

Montgomery, David L. M.D. *The Triathlon Handbook.* New York: Leisure Press, 1983.

Plant, Mike. *Iron Will: The Heart and Soul of the Triathlon's Ultimate Challenge.* Chicago: Contemporary Books, 1987.

Perry, Paul. *Paul Perry's Complete Book of the Triathlon.* New York: Plume Books, 1983.

Scott, Dave. *Dave Scott's Triathlon Training.* New York: Simon & Schuster, Inc., 1986.

Sisson, Mark with Ray Hosler. *Runner's World Triathlon Training Book.* California: Anderson World Books, 1983.

Town, Glenn P. *Science of Triathlon Training and Competition.* Illinois: Human Kinetics Publishers, Inc., 1985.

Tri-Fed/USA. *1990 Triathlon Competition Guide.* Colorado: Tri-Fed/USA, 1990.

Vaz, Katherine and Barclay Kruse. *The High-Performance Triathlete.* Chicago: Contemporary Books, 1985.

Vaz, Katherine. *Cross-Training: The Complete Book of the Triathlon.* New York: Avon Books, 1984.

WOMEN'S SPORTS BOOKS

Adrian, Marlene. *Sports Women.* New York: Karger, 1987.

Averbuch, Gloria. *The Woman Runner.* New York: Simon & Schuster, Inc., 1984.

Drinkwater, Barbara. *Female Endurance Athletes.* Champaign: Human Kinetics Publishers, 1986.

Heinonen, Janet. *Running for Women: A Complete Guide.* New York: Winner's Circle Books, 1979.

Mariolle, Elaine and Michael Shermer. *The Woman Cyclist.* Chicago: Contemporary Books, 1988.

Melpomene Institute for Women's Health Research. *The Bodywise Woman.* New York: Prentice Hall Press, 1990.

Nelson, Mariah Burton. *Are We Winning Yet?* New York: Random House, 1991.

Puhl, Jacqueline, C. Harmon Brown and Robert O. Voy. *Sports Science Perspectives For Women.* Illinois: Human Kinetics Books, 1988.

Shangold, Mona, M.D. *The Complete Sports Medicine Book For Women.* New York: Simon & Schuster, Inc., 1985.

Shangold, Mona and Gabe Mirkin. *Women and Exercise: Physiology and Sports Medicine.* Philadelphia: F.A. Davis Company, 1988.

Squires, Bill and Raymond Krise. *Improving Women's Running.* Massachusetts: The Stephen Greene Press, 1983.

Ullyot, Joan L., M.D. *Running Free: A Book for Women Runners and Their Friends.* New York: G.P. Putnam's Sons, 1980.

Wells, Christine. *Women, Sport, and Performance.* Champaign: Human Kinetics Publishers, 1985.

RESOURCE LIST

Magazines

BICYCLE GUIDE
711 Boylston Street
Boston, MA 02116
$14.90/yr. (9 issues)
800/456-6501

BICYCLING
33 E Minor Street
Emmaus, PA 18098
$17.97/yr. (10 issues)
800/441-7761

CYCLING SCIENCE
P.O. Box 1510
Mount Shasta, CA 96067
$19.97/yr. (4 issues)
916/938-4411

RUNNERS WORLD
33 E. Minor Street
Emmaus, PA 18098
$24/yr. (12 issues)
800/441-7761

RUNNING & FITNESS
9310 Old George Town Road
Bethesda, MD 20814
800/776-2732

RUNNING RESEARCH NEWS
P.O. Box 27041
Lansing, MI 48909
517/394-7953

RUNNING TIMES
P.O. Box 16927
North Hollywood, CA 91615
$18.95/yr. (12 times)
213/858-7100

SWIM MAGAZINE
P.O. Box 45497
Los Angeles, CA 90045
$19/yr. (12 times)
213/674-2120

TRIATHLETE
1415 Third Street, Suite 303
Santa Monica, CA 90401
$19.95/yr. (11 issues)
800/441-1666

TRIATHLON TODAY
P.O. Box 1587
Ann Arbor, MI 48106
$19.95/yr. (9 issues)
800/346-5902

VELONEWS
5595 Arapahoe Ave. Suite G
Boulder, CO 80303
$24.95/yr. (18 issues)
800/825-0061

WINNING
744 Roble Road
Suite 190
Allentown, PA 18103-9100
$19.95/yr. (11 issues)
800/441-1666

RESEARCH GUIDES

1990 Triathlon Competitive Guide
TRI-FED/USA
P.O. Box 1010
Colorado Springs, CO 80901
An Annual Information
Booklet

ORGANIZATIONS

Assoc. of Military Triathletes
64 Rose Hill Drive
Bluffton, SC 29910
803/757-5455

Bicycle Helmet Safety Institute
4649 Second Street S.
Arlington, VA 22204
703/521-2080

Bike Centennial
P.O. Box 8308
Missoula, MT 59807
406/721-1776

**League of American Wheelmen
(LAW)**
6706 Whitestone Rd., Suite 309
Baltimore, MD 21207
301/944-3399

**Melpomene Institute for Women's
Health Research**
1010 University Avenue
St. Paul, MN 55104
612/378-0545

**Road Runner Clubs of America
(RRCA)**
629 S. Washington Street
Alexandria, VA 22314
703/836-0558

The Athletic Congress (TAC)
P.O. Box 120
Indianapolis, IN 46206
317/638-9155

Tri-Canada
1154 W. 24th Street
N. Vancouver, BC V6V 2J2
CANADA
604/987-0092

Tri-Fed/USA
MEMBERSHIP APPLICATION
HOTLINE
800/874-1872

Tri-Fed/USA
National Office
3595 E. Fountain Blvd.
P.O. Box 1010
Colorado Springs, CO 80901
719/597-9090

Ultra Marathon Cycling Association
4790 Irvine Blvd. #105-111
Irvine, CA 92720
714/544-1701

US Amateur, Inc.
275 East Avenue
Norwalk, CT 06855
800/872-1992 or 203/866-1984

US Cycling Federation
1750 E. Boulder Street
Colorado Springs, CO 80909
719/578-4581

US Master Swimming
2 Peter Avenue
Rutland, MA 01543
505/886-6631

USOC Drug Hotline
800/223-0393

US Swimming
1750 E. Boulder
Colorado Springs, CO 80909
719/578-4578

Women's Sports Foundation
342 Madison Ave, Suite 728
New York, NY 10173
800/227-3988

TRAINING CAMPS

Camp Fleet Feet
1555 River Park Drive, Suite 102
Sacramento, CA 95815
916/442-3338

Florida Triathlon Camp
1447 Peachtree Street NE,
Suite 804
Atlanta, GA 30309
404/875-6987

John Howard School of Champions
1705 Old Mill Road
Encinitas, CA 92024
619/753-5894

Midwest Triathlon Training Camp
Jackson Y Center
127 West Wesley
Jackson, MI 49201
517/782-0537

National Triathlon Training Camp
1015 Gayley Ave., Suite 217
Los Angeles, CA 90024
213/478-8304

Triathletics Triathlon and Biathlon Training Camp
Prestige Sports
P.O. Box 937
Greenbrook, NJ 08812
800/397-1727

Tri-Texas Triathlon Training Camp
c/o THCT, 11855 1H10 West,
Suite 503
San Antonio, TX 78230

Vail Cross-Training Camp
Jim Davis
P.O. Box 3364
Vail, CO 81658
303/476-5968

NATIONAL RACE SERIES

DANSKIN TRIATHLON SERIES
111 West 40th St.
New York, NY 10018
212/764-4630

BLTS (Bud Light Triathlon Series)
5966 La Place Ct #100
Carlsbad, CA 92008
619/438-8080

IRONMAN (Hawaii) World Series Race Office
75-170 Hualalai Rd. #D214
Kailua-Kona, HI 96740
808/329-0063

IRONMAN (Hawaii)
Race Office
75-170 Hualalai Rd. #D214
Kailua-Kona, HI 96740
808/329-0063 FAX: 808/326-2131

IRONMAN Mainland Office
World Triathlon Corporation
1570 US Hwy 19N
Tarpon Springs, FL 34689
813/942-4767

RAINBO IRONKIDS Race Series
Track Sports
P.O. Box 69095
St. Louis, MO 63169
314/241-8100

100 YARDS	100 METERS	1 MILE	2000 YARDS	1.2 MILES	2000 METERS	2500 YARDS	2500 METERS	3000 YARDS	3000 METERS	2 MILES	2.4 MILES
1:00	1:06	17:36	20:00	21:07	21:52	25:00	27:20	30:00	32:49	35:12	42:14
1:05	1:11	19:04	21:40	22:53	23:42	27:05	29:37	32:30	35:33	38:08	45:46
1:10	1:17	20:32	23:20	24:28	25:31	29:10	31:54	35:00	38:17	41:04	49:16
1:15	1:22	22:00	25:00	26:24	27:20	31:15	34:11	37:30	41:01	44:00	52:48
1:20	1:27	23:28	26:40	28:08	29:10	33:20	36:27	40:00	43:45	46:56	56:19
1:25	1:33	24:56	28:20	29:55	30:59	35:25	38:44	42:30	46:29	49:52	59:50
1:30	1:38	26:24	30:00	31:41	32:49	37:30	41:01	45:00	49:13	52:48	1:03:22
1:35	1:44	27:52	31:40	33:26	34:38	39:35	43:17	47:30	51:57	55:44	1:06:53
1:40	1:49	29:20	33:20	35:12	36:27	41:40	45:34	50:00	54:41	58:40	1:10:24
1:45	1:55	30:48	35:00	36:58	38:17	43:45	47:51	52:30	57:25	1:01:36	1:13:55
1:50	2:00	32:16	36:40	38:43	40:06	45:50	50:07	55:00	1:00:09	1:04:32	1:17:26
1:55	2:06	33:44	38:20	40:29	41:55	47:55	52:24	57:30	1:02:53	1:07:28	1:20:58
2:00	2:11	35:12	40:00	42:14	43:45	50:00	54:41	1:00:00	1:05:37	1:10:24	1:24:29
2:05	2:17	36:40	41:40	44:00	45:34	52:05	56:58	1:02:30	1:08:21	1:13:20	1:28:00
2:10	2:22	36:08	43:20	54:46	47:23	54:10	59:14	1:05:00	1:11:05	1:16:16	1:31:31
2:15	2:28	39:36	45:00	47:31	49:13	56:15	1:01:31	1:07:30	1:13:49	1:19:12	1:35:03
2:20	2:33	41:04	46:40	49:17	51:02	58:20	1:03:48	1:10:00	1:16:33	1:22:08	1:38:34
2:25	2:39	42:32	48:20	51:02	52:51	1:00:25	1:06:04	1:12:30	1:19:17	1:25:04	1:42:05
2:30	2:44	44:00	50:00	52:48	54:41	1:02:30	1:08:21	1:15:00	1:22:01	1:28:00	1:45:36
2:35	2:50	45:28	51:40	54:34	56:30	1:04:35	1:10:38	1:17:30	1:24:45	1:30:56	1:49:07
2:40	2:55	46:56	53:20	56:19	58:20	1:06:40	1:12:54	1:20:00	1:27:29	1:33:52	1:52:38
2:45	3:00	48:24	55:00	58:05	1:00:09	1:08:45	1:15:11	1:22:30	1:30:13	1:36:48	1:56:10
2:50	3:06	49:52	56:40	59:50	1:01:58	1:10:50	1:17:28	1:25:00	1:32:57	1:39:44	1:59:44
2:55	3:11	51:20	58:20	1:01:36	1:03:48	1:12:55	1:19:45	1:27:30	1:35:41	1:42:40	2:03:12
3:00	3:17	52:48	1:00:00	1:03:22	1:05:37	1:15:00	1:22:01	1:30:00	1:38:26	1:45:36	2:06:43

PACE CHART—SWIMMING

MILES PER HOUR	10 MILES	20K 12.4 MILES	15 MILES	30K 18.6 MILES	20 MILES	40K 24.9 MILES	25 MILES	30 MILES	50K 31.1 MILES	40 MILES	56 * MILES	100K 62.1 MILES	75 MILES	100 MILES	112 ** MILES	150 MILES
12	:50	1:02	1:15	1:33	1:40	2:04	2:05	2:30	2:35	3:20	4:40	5:11	6:15	8:20	9:20	12:30
13	:46	:57	1:09	1:26	1:32	1:55	1:55	2:18	2:23	3:05	4:18	4:47	5:46	7:42	8:37	11:32
14	:43	:53	1:04	1:20	1:26	1:47	1:47	2:09	2:13	2:51	4:00	4:26	5:21	7:09	8:00	10:43
15	:40	:50	1:00	1:15	1:20	1:39	1:40	2:00	2:04	2:40	3:44	4:09	5:00	6:20	7:28	10:00
16	:38	:47	:56	1:10	1:15	1:33	1:34	1:53	1:57	2:30	3:30	3:53	4:41	6:15	7:00	9:23
17	:35	:44	:53	1:06	1:11	1:28	1:28	1:46	1:50	2:21	3:18	3:39	4:25	5:53	6:35	8:49
18	:33	:41	:50	1:02	1:07	1:23	1:23	1:40	1:44	2:13	3:07	3:27	4:10	5:33	6:13	8:20
19	:32	:39	:47	:59	1:03	1:18	1:19	1:35	1:38	2:06	2:57	3:16	3:57	5:16	5:54	7:45
20	:30	:37	:45	:56	1:00	1:15	1:15	1:30	1:33	2:00	2:48	3:06	3:45	5:00	5:36	7:30
21	:29	:36	:43	:53	:57	1:11	1:11	1:26	1:29	1:54	2:40	2:58	3:34	4:46	5:20	7:09
22	:27	:34	:41	:51	:55	1:08	1:08	1:22	1:25	1:49	2:33	2:49	3:25	4:33	5:05	6:49
23	:26	:32	:39	:49	:52	1:05	1:05	1:18	1:21	1:44	2:26	2:42	3:16	4:21	4:52	6:31
24	:25	:31	:38	:47	:50	1:02	1:02	1:15	1:18	1:40	2:20	2:35	3:08	4:10	4:40	6:15
25	:24	:30	:36	:45	:48	1:00	1:00	1:12	1:15	1:36	2:14	2:29	3:00	4:00	4:29	6:00
26	:23	:29	:35	:43	:46	:57	:58	1:09	1:12	1:32	2:09	2:23	2:53	3:51	4:18	5:46
27	:22	:28	:33	:41	:44	:55	:56	1:07	1:09	1:29	2:04	2:18	2:47	3:42	4:09	5:33
28	:21	:27	:32	:40	:43	:53	:54	1:04	1:07	1:26	2:00	2:13	2:41	3:34	4:00	5:21
29	:21	:26	:31	:39	:41	:51	:52	1:02	1:04	1:23	1:56	2:09	2:35	3:27	3:52	5:10
30	:20	:25	:30	:37	:40	:50	:50	1:00	1:02	1:20	1:52	2:04	2:30	3:15	3:44	5:00

* Half Ironman ** Full Ironman NOTE: Times are rounded to the nearest minute.

PACE CHART—CYCLING

MILE PACE	2 MILES	3 MILES	5 K	5 MILES	10 K	15 K	10 MILES	20 K	13.1 MILES*	15 MILES	20 MILES	26.2 MILES**
4:30	9:00	13:30	13:59	22:30	27:58	41:57	45:00	55:55	58:30	1:07:30	1:30:00	1:57:54
4:40	9:20	14:00	14:30	23:20	29:00	43:30	46:40	58:00	1:01:08	1:10:00	1:33:20	2:03:22
4:50	9:40	14:30	15:01	24:10	30:02	45:03	48:20	1:00:04	1:03:19	1:12:30	1:36:40	2:07:44
5:00	10:00	15:00	15:32	25:00	31:04	46:36	50:00	1:02:08	1:05:30	1:15:00	1:40:00	2:11:06
5:10	10:20	15:30	16:03	25:50	32:06	48:09	51:40	1:04:12	1:07:41	1:17:30	1:43:20	2:15:28
5:20	10:40	16:00	16:34	26:40	33:08	49:42	53:20	1:06:17	1:09:52	1:20:00	1:46:40	2:19:50
5:30	11:00	16:30	17:05	27:30	34:10	51:15	55:00	1:08:21	1:12:03	1:22:03	1:50:00	2:24:12
5:40	11:20	17:00	17:36	28:20	35:12	52:48	56:40	1:10:25	1:14:14	1:25:00	1:53:20	2:28:34
5:50	11:40	17:30	18:07	29:10	36:14	54:21	58:20	1:12:30	1:16:25	1:27:30	1:56:40	2:32:56
6:00	12:00	18:00	18:39	30:00	37:17	55:56	1:00:00	1:14:34	1:18:36	1:30:00	2:00:00	2:37:19
6:10	12:20	18:30	19:10	30:50	38:19	57:29	1:01:40	1:16:38	1:20:47	1:32:30	2:03:20	2:41:41
6:20	12:40	19:00	19:41	31:40	39:22	59:03	1:03:20	1:18:42	1:22:58	1:35:00	2:06:40	2:46:03
6:30	13:00	19:30	20:12	32:30	40:24	1:00:36	1:05:00	1:20:47	1:25:09	1:37:30	2:10:00	2:50:25
6:40	13:20	20:00	20:43	33:20	41:26	1:02:09	1:06:40	1:22:51	1:27:20	1:40:00	2:13:20	2:54:47
6:50	13:40	20:30	21:14	34:10	42:28	1:03:42	1:08:20	1:24:55	1:29:31	1:42:30	2:16:40	2:59:09
7:00	14:00	21:00	21:45	35:00	43:30	1:05:15	1:10:00	1:27:00	1:31:42	1:45:00	2:20:00	3:03:03
7:10	14:20	21:30	22:16	35:50	44:32	1:06:48	1:11:40	1:29:04	1:33:53	1:47:30	2:23:20	3:07:55
7:20	14:40	22:00	22:47	36:40	45:34	1:08:21	1:13:20	1:31:08	1:36:04	1:50:00	2:26:40	3:12:17
7:30	15:00	22:30	23:18	37:30	46:36	1:09:54	1:15:00	1:33:12	1:38:15	1:52:30	2:30:00	3:16:39
7:40	15:20	23:00	23:49	38:20	47:38	1:11:27	1:16:40	1:35:17	1:40:26	1:55:00	2:33:20	3:21:01
7:50	15:40	23:30	24:20	39:10	48:40	1:13:00	1:18:20	1:37:21	1:42:37	1:57:30	2:36:40	3:25:23
8:00	16:00	24:00	24:51	40:00	49:42	1:14:33	1:20:00	1:39:25	1:44:48	2:00:00	2:40:00	3:29:45
8:10	16:20	24:30	25:22	40:50	50:44	1:16:06	1:21:40	1:41:29	1:46:59	2:02:30	2:43:20	3:34:07
8:20	16:40	25:00	25:53	41:40	51:46	1:17:39	1:23:20	1:43:34	1:49:10	2:05:00	2:46:40	3:28:29
8:30	17:00	25:30	26:24	42:30	52:48	1:19:12	1:25:00	1:45:38	1:51:21	2:07:30	2:50:00	3:42:51
8:40	17:20	26:00	26:56	43:20	53:50	1:20:45	1:26:40	1:47:42	1:52:40	2:10:00	2:53:20	3:47:13
8:50	17:40	26:30	27:27	44:10	54:52	1:22:18	1:28:20	1:49:47	1:55:43	2:12:30	2:56:40	3:51:35
9:00	18:00	27:00	27:58	45:00	55:54	1:23:51	1:30:00	1:51:51	1:57:54	2:15:00	3:00:00	3:56:00
9:10	18:20	27:30	28:29	45:50	56:56	1:25:24	1:31:40	1:53:55	2:00:05	2:17:30	3:03:20	4:00:22
9:20	18:40	28:00	29:00	46:40	57:58	1:26:57	1:33:20	1:55:59	2:02:16	2:20:00	3:06:40	4:04:44
9:30	19:00	28:30	29:31	47:30	59:00	1:28:30	1:35:00	1:58:04	2:04:27	2:22:30	3:10:00	4:09:06
9:40	19:20	29:00	30:02	48:20	1:00:02	1:30:03	1:36:40	2:00:08	2:06:38	2:25:00	3:13:20	4:13:28
9:50	19:40	29:30	30:33	49:10	1:01:04	1:31:36	1:38:20	2:02:12	2:08:49	2:27:30	3:16:40	4:17:50

* Half Marathon   ** Full Marathon

PACE CHART—RUNNING

SALLY EDWARDS

Founder & President
FLEET FEET, Incorporated, a national franchise corporation with 40 retail sports stores.

Author

Triathlons for Women (1992)

Triathlons for Fun (1992)

Triathlons for Kids (1992)

The Triathlon Training and Racing Book (1985)

The Equilibrium Plan (1987)

Triathlon: A Triple Fitness Sport (1982)

The Woman Runner's Training Diary (1983)

Syndicated Columnist
Sally Edwards' Women's Sports Column.

Professional Athlete
Current Master's Ironman World Record Holder and thirteen-time Ironman Triathlon finisher.

Olympic Marathon trials Qualifier—1984.

Winner of the 1980 Western States 100-mile run and three-time finisher.

Three-time winner of the Levi Ride and Tie.

Winner of the American River 50 Miler (1980 and 1983).

Journalist
Over 100 magazine articles published.

Television Personality
KXTV-CBS television special sports commentator.

PM Magazine national special feature "Sally Edwards, The Woman Who Runs 100 Miles."

Spokesperson
Danskin Women's Triathlon Series Spokesperson (1990–91, 1991–92)

NIKE, Inc. sponsored athlete

General Foods national media tour 1984 and 1985

Academic Degrees
National University in Business (M.B.A., 1986) University of California, Berkeley, Exercise Physiology (M.A., 1970)

Memberships
Trustee, Women's Sports Foundation

Woman's Forum

Personal
After completing graduate school in Berkeley, Sally served with the American Red Cross in Vietnam. Returning home in 1972, she taught for three years before taking her entrepreneurial spirit forward and co-founding *FLEET FEET SPORTS.* Today, at the age of 44, she resides in Sacramento, California, living the fitness lifestyle as an athlete, businesswoman, author, journalist, and professional speaker.

International Triathlon Union Women's
COMMISSION

Resolutions: The Women's Commission presented the following resolutions to Congress:

a) Be it resolved that NGBs[1] be requested to appoint a liaison member (male or female) to work with the ITU Women's Commission, and to set up a Women's Committee to continue the development of "Women in Triathlon" in their own country.
   Carried Unanimously

b) Be it resolved that NGBs selecting National Teams for ITU sanctioned competitions **should** choose and equally fund (whether partially or fully) an equal number of women and men. And that this principle should be applied to age group teams whenever possible.
   Carried Unanimously

c) Be it resolved that NGBs be encouraged to develop support for "Women in Triathlon," in particular their National Women's Only Triathlons, training camps and coaching course.
   Carried Unanimously

d) Whereas the principle of equal prize money in terms of depth and amount has not been adhered to by some race organizers, be it resolved that ITU urge NGBs to comply with this principle for all NGB sanctioned competitions, and particularly at Regional and National Championships.
   Carried Unanimously

e) Whereas enormous efforts have been made to ensure the fullest equality for women in the 1990 Triathlon World Championships, i.e., separate wave start, separate finish, etc., and whereas we would like to congratulate the race director and the Organizing Committee of Tri-Fed/USA for creating these conditions, be it resolved that future ITU sanctioned competitions be required to implement the same criteria for future Triathlon World Championships.
   Carried Unanimously

f) Be it resolved that a new Executive Board position be created for a woman, and further that the Women's Commission be permitted to

---

[1] National Governing Bodies (NGB's)

nominate a person for that position, and further the Congress also be permitted to do so, and that it be for a one (1) year term only.
Carried: 31 in favour, 3 against

g) Be it resolved that the Women's Commission have the right to two (2) delegates at Congress with voice and no vote.
Carried Unanimously

h) Whereas the Executive Board has approved a budget of $1,000 to the Women's Commission, be it resolved that a further sum of $1500.00 be granted.
Carried Unanimously